CW00766674

Management Mantras

Management Mantras

S. Ramaratnam

D.K. Printworld (P) Ltd.
New Delhi

Cataloging in Publication Data — DK
[Courtesy: D.K. Agencies (P) Ltd. <docinfo@dkagencies.com>]

Ramaratnam, S. (Subramaniam), 1946 -
Management Mantras / S. Ramaratnam.
p. cm.
Includes bibliographical references (p.).
Includes index.
ISBN 13: 9788124605462
ISBN 10: 8124605467

1. Management in literature. 2. Sanskrit literature — History and criticism. I. Title.

DDC 891.2093553 22

© Author
First published in India, 2010
ISBN 13: 978-81-246-0546-2 (Pbk) ISBN 10: 81-246-0546-7

All rights reserved. No part of this publication may be reproduced or transmitted in any form or by any means, electronic or mechanical, including photocopying, recording, or any information storage or retrieval system, without prior written permission of the copyright holder, indicated above, and the publishers.

Published and printed by:
D.K. Printworld (P) Ltd.
Regd. office : *'Srikunj'*, F-52, Bali Nagar
Ramesh Nagar Metro Station
New Delhi – 110 015
Phones : (011) 2545 3975; 2546 6019; *Fax* : (011) 2546 5926
E-mail: indology@dkprintworld.com
Web: www.dkprintworld.com

Dedicated to
My Spiritual Guru
Jagadguru Shri Kripaluji Maharaj

Foreword

As India marches its way into the firmament of nations, discarding the stupor of nine hundred years of foreign rule, the glory of its ancient past is increasingly coming to light. Western scholars have often acknowledged that the Vedic texts contain the loftiest philosophic concepts known to humankind. The German philosopher Paul Deussen expressed this vividly: "Eternal philosophic truth has seldom found a more striking and decisive expression than in the emancipating knowledge of the Upanishads." However, it is now Indian scholars who are emerging to reveal the awesome secular wisdom that is also embedded in the ancient Vedic literature.

After the redemption and popularization of Vedic Mathematics, it is now the turn of Vedic Management. On reading *Management Mantras*. I was immediately reminded of Henry David Thoreau's words: "I daily bathe my intellect in the timeless wisdom of the Gītā. It is as if an empire speaks to me." This book is like a treasure house of centuries of wisdom from the ancient Indian civilization speaking to us on the theme of Management Science. Whether one is questing for tips to hone one's managerial acumen, or searching for gems of practical wisdom in life, or merely an admirer of the Vedic culture, there is enough material in it to satisfy everyone.

The book has been perfectly structured to handle this complex topic. First, the different aspects of Management Science are outlined. Then in each aspect, the modern perspective of management is described. Then, the existence and utilization of these concepts by the ancients is revealed. And finally, by diving deep into the Sanskrit literature and coming up with invaluable pearls, our understanding of these concepts is augmented with ancient wisdom. All this is done with hundreds of Sanskrit quotations, and their English translations, leaving no doubt in the minds of the reader about the brilliance of the Saints and Masters of ancient India, who packed such knowledge into their books.

This groundbreaking research could only have been accomplished by someone with both profound theoretical knowledge of Sanskrit literature and also practical appreciation of the Management process. The mantle fitted perfectly on Dr Ramaratnam, who excelled in his early academic career as a teacher of Sanskrit literature, and later branched into Management Science, to become a professor of the same. His experience in the administration of educational institutions also lent him the practical insight to do justice to this multifaceted and byzantine topic. *Vidya dadāti vinayam* — "The symptom of true knowledge is that it fosters humility. "An epitome of humility and modesty, Dr Ramaratnam is truly a remarkable scholar of present times, with full appreciation of the modern thought processes, and a deep pride in the heritage of the culture he was born in.

Swami Mukundananda
President, Jagadguru Kripalu Yog Trust

Preface

In the academic world, the dictum that remains relevant for all times is "Publish or Perish." But the magnitude of the problems of writing a book looms large only when one starts attempting the project. The limitation of time is a big constraint, especially, for the Vice-Chancellor of a university. In spite of all these problems, if I could complete the project, it was only due to the grace of the God Almighty to whom I bow down my head will all reverence.

Having concentrated upon teaching and research only for the first 20 years in my career it dawned on me later that an academician also becomes an administrator during some part of his/her life. I had the opportunity to teach several subjects but a study of *Arthaśāstra* was a kind of revelation for me. The text is quite relevant to the modern times in terms of administration and management. A few years back I got emboldened to do MBA (Part-time) as a regular candidate of the University of Madras. The subjects and the books that I studied during the course revealed that there are several parallels in Sanskrit literature on many important concepts of management. I started presenting papers on the principles of management like communication as seen from Sanskrit sources and other related themes at several conferences and seminars. A considerable part of the present work is the revised version of the papers presented in seminars and conferences.

In 12 chapters, the work touches upon the main concepts of management and their parallels from Sanskrit sources. A word of caution is necessary here. This is not a textbook on management and so some of the topics discussed in the management books may not find a place here. Only such topics that have a bearing on Sanskrit literature alone are highlighted. The book is written with the general reader in mind and so the Sanskrit content is kept at a minimum level as is necessary for the topic on hand. A general account of the topics is given in Introduction (Chapter 1).

The book is entitled as *Management Mantras* quite appropriately since the field of management today, beset with scams and corruptions needs a new direction. The word *mantra* has become quite popular of late and it is used in the sense of 'concept' or 'motto.' The word is actually a synthesis of two roots, *man* to 'think deeply' and *tra*, 'to protect.' The management in every sphere of activity needs a plunge into the thoughts on the right path and they have to be guarded against temptations of quick money or quick results even by resorting to unjustified means.

The most important management *mantra* that needs to be cultivated by all the stakeholders of business is: "the means have to be as noble as the end." Such lofty ideals were the hallmark of Indian society even till the end of the 19th century when people respected the tradition and culture drawn from the scriptures and literature. The present book is a small step towards bringing back the noble ideals of the past for the benefit of the society.

A comparative study like this requires constant updating. The author invites suggestions from management experts as well as from Sanskrit scholars for further improvement of the work. If the work kindles some interest among younger scholars to take to comparative studies for their research, the efforts of the present writer will be adequately rewarded.

S. Ramaratnam

Publishers' Note

Dr Ramaratnam brought to us the manuscript of his book on management principles in ancient literature coincidentally at a time when the Copenhagen talks about climate change were the topic of the day. As the discussions, covered in the book, on every aspect of management like decision making, human resource development and social responsibility had relevance to climate and environment, we decided to take up the publication of the work immediately.

When we wanted to select a suitable title for the work, Dr Ramaratnam came up with as many as 80 titles and after a thorough discussion it was decided to select the title 'Management Mantras'.

Science and Technology have made rapid progress in the last 100 years but they have also brought multifarious problems for which there seems to be no solution. The world is grappling with the problems of energy crisis, depletion of resources, ecological imbalance and environmental hazards. Over-exploitation of nature will cause nature's fury for which man will not be able to find a solution. As suggested by the author in various places in the book man will have to go back to the ancient wisdom for a solution. The principles of *dharma* and *karma* have strong basis and are relevant for all times. Man must learn to reduce his wants and desires and respect nature. Materialism and consumerism carried to extremes will only lead to chaos and catastrophe. As stated in the *Mahabharata* all accumulations will only end in depletion and all those that rise will have to have a fall. One should transcend selfish tendencies and offer something to the society at large with a spirit of service and sacrifice. Human values are more important than the lopsided economic progress. Man should "live and let (others) live" (with decency) and should imbibe the spirit of seeing the whole world as one family — *Vasudhaiva Kutumbakam.*

Ancient Indian philosophy has made giant strides in studying human psychology and the book discusses many of them under different headings. It is hoped that this will serve as a guide book for all those who are looking for value-oriented management which is the need of the hour.

Contents

Abbreviations

Abhi	-	*Abhijñāna-Śākuntalam*
BSS	-	Banaras Sanskrit Series
C	-	The *Mahābhārata* condensed
CSS	-	Chowkhamba Sanskrit Series
Gītā	-	*Bhagavad-Gītā*
Kir	-	*Kirātārjunīyam*
Ku	-	*Kumārasambhavam*
Manu	-	*Manu-Smṛti*
NS Press	-	Nirnaya Sagar Press
Raghu	-	*Raghuvaṁśa*
Rāmāyaṇa	-	*Vālmīki Rāmāyaṇa*
Śiśu	-	*Śiśupālavadha*
Su	-	*Subhāṣita Ratna Bhāṇḍāgāra*
Uttara	-	*Uttara Rāmacarita*

Acknowledgement

AT the outset I would like to submit my humble pranams at the lotus feet of Jagadguru Shri Kripaluji Maharaj whom I consider as my spiritual guru. Just after a darsan of Maharajji all things started moving in the right direction and the publication of the book also became a reality.

I am beholden to Swami Mukundanandaji Maharaj who is showering all his grace on me and has made me what I am today. The Foreword he has written for the book adds a special value to it.

I place on record my grateful thanks to the former Vice-Chancellor of Madras University, Dr S.P. Thyagarajan, who initiated the scheme of publishing 150 books to mark the 150th Anniversary of the Madras University. The scheme actually motivated me to write this book and it was also accepted for publication but for various reasons, it could not come out through the Press.

I am, therefore, doubly grateful to D.K. Printworld and particularly to its Director, Sri Susheel K. Mittal who came forward to publish the work. Our friendship goes beyond the Publisher–Author relationship as we have mutual respect for each other. He is doing a great service to Indian culture by bringing out useful volumes that bear the stamp of his class.

I express my heartfelt thanks to my former colleague Prof.

Padmini Mohan of T.S. Narayanaswami College, Chennai who not only helped me in proof-reading the entire work but also suggested better readings at several places in the work. I thank the members of my family for their encouragement throughout the preparation of this volume.

S. Ramaratnam

Transliteration System
With a Guide to Pronunciation

	As	As in		As	As in
a	a	arise	c	ch	charity
ā	a	arm	ch	ch	catch-him
i	i	image	ja	ju	jug
ī	ea	eat	jha	dgeh	hedge-hog
u	u	put	ñ	n	punch
ū	u	Pluto	ṭa	tu	tuck
ṛ	r	rhythm	ṭh	th	ant-hill
e	e	Begum	ḍa	do	done
ai	i	ice	ḍh	dh	god-head
o	o	oral	ṇ	n	plunder
au	ow	owl	ta	tho	thorough
ka	ka	kafir	tha	thu	thumb
kha	ckh	blockhead	da	tha	that
ga	ga	garden	dha	thah	breath-here
gha	gha	aghast	na	nu	nun
ṅ	n	gang			

	As	As in
pa	pu	pub
ph	ph	phoo-phoo
ba	bu	bun
bh	bh	abhor
ma	mu	mug
ya	yo	young
ra	ru	rut
la	lu	luck
va	vu	vulcano
śa	sa	darsan
ṣa	shu	shut
sa	su	sun
ha	hu	hug

1

Introduction

Management as a Study

MANAGEMENT science has developed as a major subject of study in the past few decades. Trade and business have been carried on by people all over the world from time immemorial but a scientific study of the business concepts has taken shape only from the nineteenth century. In common terms, the word "management" is generally associated with business though it has wide application in almost every field of human activity. Everyone needs to take care of one's own physical, mental, intellectual and spiritual development. A good management of one's own needs, that is, basic, security, social, self-esteem and self-actualization, can put things in a proper perspective and help one to fix up the priorities in life. It is a matter of common experience that a planned approach takes one near to the desired goals while aimless wandering leads one nowhere. Management of men, material and money in private life is as much important as in business. Mismanagement of these could be disastrous; more particularly so in business since it affects a large number of stakeholders. Though management is all about planning and co-ordination, a large number of finer aspects of management need to be studied, analysed and applied in the present-day context of liberalization, privatization and globalization. A small decision may have a far-reaching influence in the professional world.

There is a need, therefore, to enlarge the scope of a field like management. Life is a cycle; old fashions get revived; even old wine is acceptable if it is packed in a new bottle. Fresh light is to be thrown on old concepts and principles so that they become valid and acceptable.

The *Ṛgveda* says, "Let noble thoughts come to us from all directions."[1] Principles of management as available in Sanskrit sources, be it a technical work like *Arthaśāstra*, a literary work like *Śākuntalam* or a philosophical work like the *Bhagavad-Gītā* can be helpful to administrators and businessmen. The concepts of *dharma, artha, kāma* and *mokṣa* are quite relevant even today.

Like a majority of the fields, management study can be approached from different angles like mathematical, statistical, theoretical, practical, and so on. The ultimate aim is, therefore, to see how far the approach benefits the individual and the society at large. The principles though theoretically well defined, yet need slight modification and orientation depending upon the field chosen, the place of operation and the state of the society. A management student might have excelled in his/her studies in Harvard Business School but he/she will find that 50 per cent of what he/she had studied may not be applicable to the conditions in India. He/She has to innovate and change his/her approach as suited to the conditions prevailing. A doctor, for example, might have had his/her training in the most scientific manner but he/she must also know-how to apply a medical procedure suitable to the conditions of a particular patient. In the application of management concepts with respect to the conditions in India, the traditional values and principles will be of immense help

---

1. आ नो भद्राः क्रतवो यन्तु विश्वतः।
ā no bhadrāḥ kratavo yantu viśvataḥ।
— *Ṛgveda*, I.89.1.

in solving the problems of administration. A number of ideas that are enshrined in literature may find their application in the present-day situation as well.

Kālidāsa says, "A wise man favours one or the other method after proper examination, while a fool is carried away by the opinion of others."[2]

Management Study and Decision Making

Management does not mean simply managing the affairs in a given situation. A manager has to involve himself/herself in the decision-making environment. The history of an organization, its background, financial and material resources, human resources, political situation and many such factors have to be taken into consideration while taking decisions. In spite of a fairly good analysis of all these factors, decisions can still go wrong. But the analysis will be helpful in finding out where it went wrong and in taking the remedial measures. Decision making should always be preceded by back-up measures to provide a cushion if the decision were to go wrong. So says a Subhāṣita (a pithy saying on morals/values/worldly vision): "One should think of the remedial measures anticipating a mishap. It is not wise to dig a well when the house is ablaze with fire."[3]

---

2. सन्तः परीक्ष्यान्यतरद्भजन्ते
   मूढः परप्रत्ययनेयबुद्धिः।
   santaḥ parīkṣyānyataradbhajante
   mūḍhaḥ parapratyayaneyabuddhiḥ ||
   — *Mālavikāgnimitra*, I.2

3. चिन्तनीया हि विपदामादावेव प्रतिक्रिया।
   न हि कूपखननं युक्तं प्रदीप्ते वह्निना गृहे।।
   cintanīyā hi vipadāmādāveva pratikriyā |
   na hi kūpakhananaṁ yuktaṁ pradīpte vahninā gṛhe ||
   — *Śārṅgadharapaddhati*, v. 1440

Management and Communication

Every area of management, like planning, co-ordination and decision making, needs effective communication. Unless the plans are communicated, their execution cannot take place. Co-ordination involves effective communication among all those concerned in an establishment. Likewise, it is absolutely essential to convey the decisions taken. The present age is called Information Age; there are facilities like desktop video-conferencing, cell phones and Internet that have revolutionized the communication systems. All these have also put more pressure on the communication skill of the managers. Companies advertise saying that they want candidates irrespective of their degree provided they have good communication skills. However, communication skill cannot be developed overnight. It needs a special kind of training. Here again, a study of literature will be helpful in identifying the marks of good communication and developing them. Verbal testimony has been accorded a very high status in Sanskrit technical literature and it deals with the concepts of communication quite extensively.

Human Resource Management

Machine and money can be effectively managed by a clever manager. But management of the human resources is more difficult because of the varied behavioural patterns of human beings. Yes; human beings are subject to feelings or emotions which money and machine do not have. Management of human beings is complex on account of the emotional factor. The same person behaves differently under different situations; hence individual behaviour and group behaviour have to be studied independently. The speed of a machine can be increased or decreased by the tightening or loosening of a few bolts and nuts but human behaviour cannot be altered like that. Human brain and human energy have enormous powers that cannot be matched by hundreds of machines. Hence, the human resource, if handled deftly, is a veritable source of power and prosperity. Indian poets and thinkers have made giant strides on the study of human resource and human psychology and therefore their guidance will be of immense help to the present-day managers.

Centres of Power

Every organization has centres of power and authority. Without authority, administration becomes slack and ineffective. Every official has to exercise his/her power to get things done. But power must be used judiciously. Absolute power corrupts absolutely. If the power goes into the head of an individual who cannot handle it properly, it will be disastrous to the entire society. Exercising power is like walking on a thin rope. Power is a double-edged sword. It has to be handled carefully. It is in this respect that literature comes very handy. It teaches us how to handle power without injuring others and without hurting oneself. One should function with an accent on *dharma,* without fear or favour, without pride or prejudice. It is more easily said than done but lives of great personalities will be a pointer in this direction.

Leadership

Swami Vivekananda says that the history of the world is dominated by a few persons who had faith in themselves. He has thus emphasized that the hallmark of a leader lies in self-belief or self-confidence. A manager is essentially a leader and unless a person shows leadership qualities he/she cannot become a manager. Leadership may be defined as an influence exercised in a situation and directed through the communication process toward the attainment of a specialized goal. A leader is expected to possess emotional stability to deal with situations. He/She should be ready to shoulder responsibilities and find solutions to the problems faced. He/She should set an example for others by leading from the front through his/her own performance. He/She should be sympathetic toward his/her subordinates, yet firm in his/her dealings. There are different types of leadership like autocratic leadership and democratic leadership. Sanskrit literature is a veritable source book on leadership qualities.

Team Spirit

A manager generally operates in a group. A single manager or a group of managers alone cannot function in isolation. Supervisors, workers and other support staff form the majority of the human power in an organization. It is the duty of a manager to build a team and work in co-ordination with everybody in the team. It requires enormous managerial skill to build a team. It is often said that a team is only as good as its members. Even so, a team leader can motivate his/her team members to give a better performance. He/She has to delegate powers to the team members and supervise their performance. He/She has to invite their opinion on specific problems and listen to their views patiently. Mere instructions generally do not carry much weight. People rise to the occasion only when some amount of responsibility is given to them. For example, on the question of accepting the surrender of Vibhīṣaṇa, Rāma listens to the views of all his team members before taking a decision. Many such instances in literature bring out the importance of team spirit.

Planning

Planning is a universal concept, the best example of which can be seen in nature. Everything in nature seems to take place in a pre-determined fashion. The onset of seasons, the blossoming of a flower, the flowing of the rivers, the waxing and waning of the moon and all such natural phenomena have a set pattern. The entire evolution seems to move ahead in a planned manner. A planned approach takes one to the desired goal more easily and quickly than an unplanned one. Planning is an essential aspect of management; planning is all about preparing answers for the questions, "what," "why," "when," "who" and "how." The *Arthaśāstra* deals with planning quite elaborately and the points discussed in the text are applicable even to the present-day context.

Organizational Behaviour

The behaviour of a person is determined by several factors such as biological factors, cultural factors, social and environmental factors. The attitudes of individuals also play a part in their behaviour. All these need to be studied from the organizational point of view by a manager. Sanskrit philosophical texts and literature deal with the various aspects of human psychology. The behaviour of a person can be studied through his/her actions; not only physical actions but also mental actions, both of which are controlled by the three *guṇa*s, namely, *sattva, rajas* and *tamas*. A proper training to strike a balance between these three qualities can solve majority of the organizational problems.

Social Responsibility

Gone are the days when business establishments concentrated on profit making alone. With the spread of education, even common people have become aware of the environmental upkeep and ecological balance. Chemical industry and leather industry, for example, leave behind a large amount of industrial waste and toxic substances that become a threat to the lives of human beings and animals. The state and central governments have also enacted stringent rules on waste treatment. The present-day manager, thus, has a very big challenge. Even industries that do not cause pollution are expected to provide services for health care and education in the area of their operation. They have to provide employment opportunities for the local people. Companies have the responsibility of maintaining good labour relations since labour problems spill over to the entire society and affect the common people as well. There is also pressure on the managers to be transparent in their dealings since they are answerable to all those connected with the business. Business houses have a role to play to protect and nurture the art and culture of the land. They may extend a helping hand to charitable institutions and provide scholarships to poor and deserving students in the neighbourhood area. *Dāna* or charity has received significant attention in our literature.

Total Quality Management

Conceptually, Total Quality Management (TQM) is rather new but there has always been a need for it in business. The concept has assumed greater significance in the present-day scenario which is customer-centred. Where there is competition among manufacturers, there is greater emphasis not only on meeting the customer's requirement on quality but also on continuous improvement. All departments and all employees are geared up towards quality requirements. There is thus a need for effective management of quality-control measures. This is what is known as TQM. The *Arthaśāstra* contains a number of ideas that are subtly connected to this important concept.

Consumer Orientation

The market trends have changed drastically in the past few

years. It has shifted from manufacturer-centric to consumer-centric. In the 1970s and 1980s, one had to book for a quality scooter by paying an advance and wait for three or four years to get it. Now two-wheelers and four-wheelers have flooded the market. It is no more a seller's market; it is buyer's market now. Companies are forced to turn toward hitherto ignored concepts like consumer orientation and customer satisfaction. The attitudes of the consumers have also changed over the years. Earlier the price alone used to be the criterion for a customer. Now a consumer looks for quality of the goods and is prepared to spare a little more money if he/she can get quality stuff. There is also a tendency to seek a better ambience for the purchase of goods. A petty shop owner may sell a soap for Rs. 10, which a middle-class person would be happy to buy. Now he/she prefers to buy it in a shopping mall though it may cost him/her Rs. 2 more. The air-conditioned comfort and the freedom to go around and choose the product of his/her choice, facility for parking and such other factors contribute to the change in his/her attitude. The discussion on what contributes to the ultimate satisfaction of people is the central theme of many a work in literature.

Progress Coupled with a Vision

An individual must set a goal for himself/herself if he/she wants to make progress. This holds good for a company as well. A company must decide what it wants to be, what it should stand for and what its brand image should be. In short, it must have a vision and the vision should be linked to the core values of the company. A vision cannot be realized by a single person's effort. The management as well as the employees have to work hard towards the realization of the company's ideal or vision. Production of goods, their marketing, advertisement, accounting, administration and all such activities connected with a company should be oriented toward the vision. This is called the mission. If the vision is called a non-perceivable ideal, mission is the tangible target set for realizing the ideal. Mission is the means and the vision the end. All our scriptures and literature emphasize that both the means and the end should be noble. The ends do not justify the means.

While discussing the Sanskrit sources in relation to some of the management principles, it should not be misconstrued that they are the ultimate in every aspect of management. What we are going to see in the following chapters are certain guidelines that will be helpful to every manager.

Such guidelines could be seen in the large number of didactic works in the different vernaculars. For example, the *Tirukkuraḷ* in Tamil is an excellent work on several aspects of management. A comparative study of modern management concepts and the elements of the same available in literature will indeed be a rewarding experience.

2

Decision Making

The Need for Decision Making

PROBLEMS are generally twofold, namely, those created by human beings and those that are beyond their control, each of which has to be approached in a different way. Problems remain problems only as far as they are not countered directly. A wise person faces the problems and tries to solve them while a fool broods over them and laments. A manager should anticipate problems and be ready with solutions. Quick decisions have to be taken while facing unexpected problems and that is where the management skill of a person lies. Decision making covers almost every aspect of management:[1]

(i) As a planner, a manager has to devise steps to achieve the objectives of the company.

---

1. (i) Management is nothing but decision making — H.H. Simon, p. 1.
   (ii) Almost everything managers do involves decision making, — G.R. Terry, p. 66.
   (iii) Decision making is closely related to planning — N.H. Newman, C.E. Summer, and E.K. Warren, chapter 2.
   (iv) Decision making is the core of Management planning — Koontz, Harold and Cyril O'Donnell, *Elements of Management*, p. 89.
   (v) Managers are evaluated on the basis of number and importance of decisions made — Gleuck, p. 384

(ii) As an organizer, a manager has to choose horses for courses, that is, to select suitable persons for the respective jobs and assign the jobs to them.

(iii) As a leader, the manager has to motivate the subordinates and integrate their efforts.

(iv) As an authority, the manager has to exercise control over material and human resources.

Decisions may have to be taken sometimes in a crunch situation, but majority of decisions are made after careful planning. A decision represents a judgement; a final resolution on a conflict of needs, means or goals; and a commitment to action made in the face of uncertainty, complexity and even irrationality.[2]

Definition of Decision Making

Decision making may be defined as the process by which individuals select a course of action from among alternatives to produce a desired result. It has four stages: explorative (searching), speculative (analysing), evaluative (weighing options) and selective (commitment).[3]

In the exploratory stage, the origin of a particular problem is searched for. If the root cause of the problem is understood, half of the problem is already solved. In the speculative stage, an analysis is made on the options available for solving the problem. In the evaluative stage, all the available options are weighed from several angles. For some of the problems, cost effectiveness has to be looked into. Some problems are to be solved irrespective of the cost involved. In the final stage, a choice is made among the options available based on careful analysis in order to maximize the benefits and minimize the risks.

---

2. M. Lopez Felix, p. 73.
3. F.A. Shull Jr., A.L. Delebecq and L. Cummings, p. 31.

The four stages mentioned above are essential steps since decisions should not be taken on the spur of a moment. Some problems may get solved automatically in course of time with the administrator doing nothing at all. These are only per-chance occasions; decisions cannot always be left to chance. It is therefore necessary for a manager to go through the four stages. How quickly he has to do it, depends on the demands of the situation. A manager has to look for alternative solutions to problems. If there is only one solution to a problem, there is no scope for decision making and no manager is required to handle such a situation. The CEO can manage it by himself.

Types of Decisions

Books on management talk of three types of decisions.

BASIC AND ROUTINE DECISIONS

Basic and routine decisions are repetitive in nature. There will generally be a set of rules and regulations to be followed in taking such decisions. For example, in a situation like an employee exceeding his quota of leave, the wages are cut for the number of days exceeded. There is no need for deliberating on such cases. On the other hand, if an employee has met with an accident and if he has no medical leave to his credit, the management may take a decision to waive the days of absence and pay wages. In non-routine cases like expanding a plant, decisions have to be taken after a careful analysis. Managers have to take strategic decisions at times. On such occasions, managers have to keep in mind the goals and ideals of the organization. According to Drucker, the higher the level in the management hierarchy, the greater is the responsibility of a manager in making strategic decisions.[4]

---

4. Peter F. Drucker, p. 352.

PERSONAL AND IMPERSONAL DECISIONS

While talking about personal decisions, we are not generally concerned about those decisions that affect only a particular individual, as for example, to buy a flat or an independent house. However, in an official/professional setting, there emerge decisions that have some element of personal involvement in official work. For example, there could be a general understanding that dignitaries visiting a company are provided accommodation in a five-star hotel. But a manager looking after the arrangement may have a preference for a particular hotel (perhaps, in view of its proximity) where a personal element plays a part. But there are a number of decisions that are concerned with shareholders, customers, dealers or general public where there is no scope for any personal element. Thus the decisions taken by managers have a far-reaching influence on several stakeholders. According to Levitt,[5] a manager is judged not for what he/she knows about the work, but how well he/she actually does the work. A manager is always under pressure to perform. If everything goes well, nobody will utter a word but if something goes wrong everybody will condemn him/her. It is therefore necessary for a manager to infuse a professional approach in his/her decision-making style.[6]

PROGRAMMED AND UN-PROGRAMMED DECISIONS

With the increased use of computers in all fields, decision making can also be done through machines through programmed software. In certain areas like chemical industry, the production cannot be stopped abruptly. In such cases, a programmed decision is taken on the purchase of raw material.

5. Theodre Levitt, p. 120.
6. F.B. Flippo, and G.M. Munninger, p. 99.

Situations that are of non-recurring nature and those that are unique need a lot of reflection and discussion. There will be no instant solution to such problems because one cannot anticipate them and keep ready a programmed solution. Also the same problem will need different approaches at different times. For example, the proposal to shift the company to a more spacious place needs a lot of deliberation. Ultimately, a decision may be taken not to shift the company at all. Such decisions are un-programmed decisions.

The Decision-Making Process

Decisions may be taken quickly or after much deliberation. However, there should be a process in all decision-making exercises. Sanskrit rhetoricians speak of two ways by which the suggested meaning of an expression appeals to a discerning reader; one is called *samlakṣya-krama vyaṅgya,* where the process of evolution of the suggested meaning is clearly seen. The other one is *asamlakṣya-krama vyaṅgya,* where the process is so quick that it is hardly perceived. An illustration is given for this process. It is like piercing a bunch of a hundred lotus leaves with a needle. The moment the needle is pressed on the first leaf it is through to the last leaf. The needle passes through each and every leaf but the process is hardly recognizable. Likewise, certain decisions are taken so quickly that the process is hardly recognizable but the process has to be gone through in any case. The important steps to be taken in decision making are:

(i) At the first stage, an awareness of the problem is created. Here, the emphasis is on knowing what the problem is rather than thinking of a solution;

(ii) In the next stage the problem is diagnosed. Here the root cause of the problem is analysed;

(iii) In the third stage, all possible solutions are analysed;

(iv) In the next stage, the possible solutions are evaluated and short-listed;

(v) In the penultimate stage, the best among the short-listed solutions is chosen, taking into consideration the economy of effort, risks involved, timing and limitation of the resources; and

(vi) In the last stage the decision is implemented and follow-up measures are taken.

Sanskrit Sources on Decision Making

Kauṭilya discusses the causes of calamities in a state, exclusively in the Eighth Chapter of *Arthaśāstra*. While facing calamities, an administrator has to take quick decisions. The *Arthaśāstra* gives a list of five steps for decision making. They are:

मन्त्रो मन्त्रफलप्राप्तिः कर्मानुष्ठानं
आयव्ययकर्म दण्डप्रणयनं
अमित्राटवीप्रतिषेधो राज्यरक्षणं
व्यसनप्रतीकारः . . .।

mantro mantraphalaprāptiḥ karmānuṣṭhānaṁ
āyavyayakarma daṇḍapraṇayanaṁ
amitrāṭavīpratiṣedho rājyarakṣaṇaṁ
vyasanapratīkāraḥ . . .।

— *Arthaśāstra*, 8.1.8

(1) Deliberation in counsel,
(2) Securing the fruits of deliberation,
(3) Carrying out undertakings,
(4) Managing income and expenditure, and
(5) Taking steps against a possible setback.

Kauṭilya gives a series of case studies and provides solutions to them. Many of them may not have a bearing on the present-day situation but still they are worth noting for the methodology adopted.

For example, calamities may befall the treasury and the army at the same time. Which would be attended to first? As a *prima facie* view, Kauṭilya first states the opinion of one Kauṇapadanta, who says that the calamity on the army is more serious and therefore it must be attended to first, for, the subjugation of enemies is dependent on the army. If the army is neglected, the enemies will take advantage of it and the loss of treasury becomes imminent. The calamity of the treasury can be overcome by the seizure of the enemy's land with the help of the army and treasury can be supplemented by the revenue got from the enemy's land.

Kauṭilya rejects this view and establishes that army is rooted in the treasury. In the absence of treasury, there will be no money to pay the armymen who will switch over to the enemy's side. With the treasury given due care, it is easy to raise an army. Kauṭilya, however, says that army or treasury becomes important in the light of place, time and work.

According to Vātavyādhi, between the calamities befalling the army and the ally, the calamity of the ally is more serious. The ally may help us without expecting money immediately and with his help we can drive away the enemy and save our army.

Kauṭilya rejects this view as well. According to him, when one has a strong army, the ally remains firm and the enemy will also offer peace. Therefore, the problems concerning the army must be attended to first. However, in a work that can be well performed either by the army or by the ally, advantage comes from their relative strength and the attainment of suitable place and time. But an ally is of no avail in a speedy expedition against an enemy since one needs time to mobilize the army. If the calamity of the army continues, even an ally will try to take advantage of it and secure his own interest.

In addition to giving theoretical ideas on decision making, Kauṭilya presents some significant case studies, states the opinion of other authors and establishes his own opinion.

The *Viduranīti* portion of the *Mahābhārata* has several ideas on decision making. It speaks of six evils to be discarded by a person who works towards prosperity; they apply equally well to decision making.

षड्दोषाः पुरुषेणेह हातव्या भूतिमिच्छता।
निद्रा तन्द्री भयं क्रोधं आलस्यं दीर्घसूत्रता।।

ṣaṭdoṣāḥ puruṣeṇeha hātavyā bhūtimicchatā ।
nidrā tandrī bhayaṁ krodhaṁ ālasyaṁ dīrghasūtratā ।।

— *Vidura-Nīti*, I.85

The six evils are:

(1) excessive sleep,
(2) carelessness,
(3) laziness,
(4) fear,
(5) anger, and
(6) procrastination.

We have a very good example in the *Rāmāyaṇa* of how a decision should be taken.

Vibhīṣaṇa, Rāvaṇa's younger brother, seeks protection under Rāma. The big question is whether to accept him or not. An important and a quick decision had to be taken by Rāma. Rāma could have made the decision all by himself but he chose to consult all his trusted colleagues. Sugrīva says,

सुदुष्टेवाऽप्यदुष्टो वा किमेष रजनीचरः।
ईदृशीं व्यसनं प्राप्तं भ्रातरं यः परित्यजेत्।।
को नाम स भवेत्तस्य यमेष न परित्यजेत्।

suduṣṭovā 'pyaduṣṭo vā kimeṣa rajanīcaraḥ ।
īdṛśīṁ vyasanaṁ prāptaṁ bhrātaraṁ yaḥ parityajet ।
ko nāma sa bhavettasya yameṣa na parityajet ।
— *Vālmīki Rāmāyaṇa*, VI.18-5-6

A person who deserts his brother's side at a critical juncture should not be believed. Whom indeed will he not treacherously forsake?

Lakṣmaṇa and others were also of the same opinion. Vibhīṣaṇa probably has an ambition to usurp his elder brother's throne and become the king of Laṅkā. Moreover Vibhīṣaṇa is a *rākṣasa* and as is well known, *rākṣasa*s are deceitful. Those who have ulterior motives in an action should not be accepted as allies. But Hanumān says to Rāma: "Seeing how able and watchful you are and knowing how wicked his brother is, hearing that you killed Vāli in order to install Sugrīva and desiring to be a king which is a natural ambition, he has purposely come here."

Hanumān, though in favour of accepting Vibhīṣaṇa, does not want to deny the charge that Vibhīṣaṇa may have an idea in his mind to become a king. But there are other considerations that are stronger than this in approaching Rāma. In fact, Rāma approves Hanumān's suggestion but not before convincing people like Sugrīva, to whom he says: "Not all brothers are like Bharata, or sons like me or friends like you." These kind words would have definitely changed the mind of Sugrīva, who otherwise would have felt sore that his opinion was discarded. This is an important aspect of decision making. An administrator should listen to the ideas of others. Obviously, he/she cannot take all their suggestions. Only one may be taken and the others will have to be discarded. But a word of appreciation should be given to all those who gave their opinions and it should be explained why their suggestion could not be taken. Otherwise, they will not express their opinion in the subsequent meetings.

Rāma not only accepted Vibhīṣaṇa's offer of surrender but also promised him the *rākṣasa* kingdom. It was a bold and strategic decision. Being doubly pleased, Vibhīṣaṇa worked wholeheartedly for Rāma's victory. Rāma could also get all the details about Rāvaṇa's strengths and weaknesses from Vibhīṣaṇa. It was a diplomatic decision to accept Vibhīṣaṇa, says Kālidāsa:

> काले खलु समारब्धाः फलं बध्ननन्ति नीतयः।
> *kāle khalu samārabdhāḥ phalaṁ badhnanti nītayaḥ* ।।
> — *Raghuvaṁśa*, XII.69

> Rāma promised to him (Vibhīṣaṇa) the lordship over the *rākṣasa*s. Tactics employed at the right time bear fruit invariably.

We have an interesting scene in Kālidāsa's *Mālavikāgnimitram*. King Agnimitra is enraged at the act of the king of Vidarbha, who has imprisoned his cousin Mādhavasena, his wife and sister. Agnimitra demands that they should be released immediately. The king of Vidarbha declares that Mādhavasena would be released only if Agnimitra released his (Vidarbha king's) brother-in-law. He also says casually that Mādhavasena's sister had disappeared and that she could not be traced. According to Agnimitra, the king of Vidarbha is a natural enemy and therefore he has to be subjugated. Agnimitra therefore orders an expedition. The minister appreciates his stand and says:

अचिराधिष्ठितराज्यः शत्रुः प्रकृतिष्वरूढमूलत्वात्।
नवसंरोहणशिथिलस्तरुरिव सुकरः समुद्धर्तुम्।।

acirādhiṣṭhitarājyaḥ śatruḥ prakṛtiṣvarūḍhamūlatvāt ।
navasaṁrohaṇaśithilastaruriva sukaraḥ samuddhartum ।।
— *Mālavikāgnimitra*, I.8

An enemy who has first come to the throne and thereafter has not secured the devotion of his subjects is like a freshly planted tree that has not struck its roots deep into soil; both can be easily uprooted.

In a decision-making process, the manager should pay due attention to the views of his team members. This idea is emphasized by Bhāravi in his *Kirātārjunīyam*. The Pāṇḍavas are languishing in the forest during their exile. Meanwhile Duryodhana is consolidating his position in the kingdom. The spy says:

स किंसखा साधु न शास्ति योऽधिपं
हितान्न यः संशृणुते स किंप्रभुः।
सदानुकूलेषु हि कुर्वते रतिं
नृपेष्वमात्येषु च सर्वसम्पदः।।

sa kiṁsakhā sādhu na śāsti yo 'dhipaṁ
hitānna yaḥ saṁśṛṇute sa kiṁprabhuḥ ।।
sadānukūleṣu hi kurvate ratiṁ
nṛpeṣvamātyeṣu ca sarvasaṁpadaḥ ।।
— *Kirātārjunīya*, I.5

He is an undesirable counsellor who does not give proper advice to his master; and he is a bad master who does not listen to the counsellors; for, prosperity of every kind is delighted to attend a place where the master and the counsellors are always in perfect accord with each other.

सहसा विदधीत न क्रियामविवेकः परमापदां पदम्।
वृणुते हि विमृष्यकारिणं गुणलुब्धाः स्वयमेव संपदः।।

sahasā vidadhīta na kriyāmavivekaḥ paramāpadāṁ padam ।
vṛṇute hi vimṛṣyakāriṇaṁ guṇalubdhāḥ svayameva saṁpadaḥ ॥

— Ibid., II.30

One should not plunge into action hastily. Want of deliberation (in decision making) is a source of calamities. Fortunes that are ever attached to merits, seek, of their own accord, one who acts with proper thought.

अभिवर्षति योऽनुपालयन्विधिबीजानि विवेकवारिणा।
स सदा फलशालिनीं क्रियां शरदं लोक इवाधितिष्ठति॥

abhivarṣati yo 'nupālayanvidhibījāni vivekavāriṇā ।
sa sadā phalaśālinīṁ kriyāṁ śaradaṁ loka ivādhitiṣṭhati ॥

— Ibid., II.31

He who nourishes the seed of decisions with water of deliberation and preserving them has mastery over labour that will be rich with fruit as people (who have worked hard earlier) can control the autumn with rich harvest.

Yudhiṣṭhira, accordingly has a discussion with his brothers. It is decided that they should equip themselves to meet the challenge of the enemy. Accordingly, Arjuna performs penance and acquires a missile from Lord Śiva himself after crossing many hurdles.

A case for decision making is presented in *Śiśupālavadha* of Māgha. Kṛṣṇa wanted to destroy his enemy, namely, Śiśupāla and so preparations were made for the expedition. At the same time, there came an invitation from Yudhiṣṭhira to attend a sacrifice performed by him. Now the question is whether to go ahead with the military expedition or postpone it so that the sacrifice could be attended. A decision had to be taken. Kṛṣṇa seeks the counsel of his elder brother Balarāma and minister Uddhava. Balarāma advises that the enemy should be quelled first.

समूलघातमघ्नन्तः परान्नोद्यन्ति मानिनः।
प्रध्वंसितान्धतमसस्तत्रोदाहरण रविः॥

samūlaghātamaghnantaḥ parānnodyanti māninaḥ।
pradhvaṁsitāndhatamasastatrodāharaṇa raviḥ॥

— *Śiśupālavadha*, II.33

Men of honour are not satisfied unless the enemy is destroyed completely just as the sun that will not be satisfied without destroying darkness completely.

But Uddhava takes a different stand. He says:

सामवादाः सकोपस्य तस्य प्रत्युत दीपकाः।
प्रतप्तस्येव सहसा सर्पिषस्तोयबिन्दवः॥

sāmavādāḥ sakopasya tasya pratyuta dīpakāḥ।
prataptasyeva sahasā sarpiṣastoyabindavaḥ॥

— Ibid., II.55

When the decision to subjugate the enemy must be taken, negotiations for peace will only inflame the enemy, just as drops of water sprinkled on heated ghee (to cool it) will only blaze up in flames.

सोपधानां धियं धीराः स्थेयसीं खट्वयन्ति ये।
तत्रानिशं निषण्णास्ते जानते जातु न श्रमम्॥

sopadhānāṁ dhiyaṁ dhīrāḥ stheyasīṁ khaṭvayanti ye।
tatrāniśaṁ niṣaṇṇāste jānate jātu na śramam॥

— Ibid., II.77

Those who constantly lie on the bedstead of firm will, upholstered with sound reasoning, never know what fatigue is.

नालम्बते दैष्टिकतां न निषीदति पौरुषे।
शब्दार्थौ सत्कविरिव द्वयं विद्वानपेक्षते।।

nālambate daiṣṭikatāṁ na niṣīdati pauruṣe।
śabdārthau satkaviriva dvayaṁ vidvānapekṣate।।

— Ibid., II.86

> In decision making, mere reliance on providence will not help; raw aggressiveness will also be futile. A wise man should take the help of both, just as a good poet, possessed of learning, pays attention to both words and their sense.

After such deliberations, it is decided that Kṛṣṇa should go and attend Yudhiṣṭhira's sacrifice. Śiśupāla may also attend the same. If he causes any trouble there, he should be killed on the spot.

There are many such instances in Sanskrit literature where ideas on decision making are set forth. They may not be directly connected with the concept of decision making as we have today but relevant illustrations from literary works may add variety to the subject and make the study interesting.

3

Communication

The Importance of Communication

COMMUNICATION is an important aspect of human life. As a study it has gained prominence in recent times, with the development of management science. According to an estimate, about 75 per cent of human activity is spent in communication, speaking or writing. Most of the problems of the world can be traced to misunderstanding, which arises due to lack of communication, improper communication or wrong communication. Effective communication can bring about better interpersonal relationships. It can improve industrial relations and pave the way for optimum use of human resources. It can even bring about better international understanding and mutual faith. The ability to communicate effectively has enabled human beings to build organizations, societies and other social groupings that make for survival and better living.[1] The ideals of a company, its vision and goals have to be let known to the employees and stakeholders through proper communication. The most important task of a manager is to communicate effectively with the team members and employees. With the globalization concept gaining prominence and the channels becoming faster and pervasive,

---

1. Dalton E. McFarland, *Management Foundations and Practices,* p. 566.

communication has assumed greater importance in the present-day context. The accent is now on worldwide communication. For establishing their credibility, companies communicate through the media. Full-page advertisements in leading newspapers carry the achievement and balance sheet of companies. It is said, "out of sight, out of mind." In order to stay in the race for supremacy, a company attracts public attention through various modes of communication.

Definition of Communication

Communication is the presentation of facts and figures so as to make a person respond to an idea in the way that is intended by the speaker or a writer. Communication is not a one-way process. Unless the speaker's idea is understood correctly by the listener, the process of communication is not complete. Communication is important for dissemination of information and for conveying rules and regulations. Communication is fundamental to decision making.

Communication involves an exchange of facts, ideas, opinions or emotions of two or more people.[2] It is a process of meaningful interaction among human beings.[3] Communication is the sum of all things a person does when he/she wants to create an understanding in the mind of another. It is a bridge between the speaker and the listener. It involves a systematic and continuous process of telling, listening and understanding.[4] Communication is the broad field of human interchange of facts and opinions.[5]

---

2. Keith Davis, p. 65.
3. Dalton E. McFarland, *Management Foundations and Practices*, pp. 566-68.
4. L.A. Allen, *Management and Organization*, p. 144.
5. C.E. Redfield, *Communication in Management*, p. 3.

Communication may be upward, downward or lateral in the mode of speaking, writing, reading and of media channels or network. It is very important in the field of interpersonal, intra-organizational or inter-organizational activities.

The Role of Communication

The importance of communication is spread over almost all functions of an organization:

(i) It is helpful in the smooth functioning of managerial activities like planning, co-ordination, directing and controlling.

(ii) It is helpful in discharging one's duties and responsibilities.

(iii) It is helpful in realizing the goals of an organization.

(iv) Communication reveals the authority, position and task.

(v) Communication is helpful in getting the feedback from all those concerned.

(vi) It is the basis of decentralization and delegation of powers.

(vii) It is the prime process of democratization in a company.

(viii) It binds people together and boosts the morale of the employees.

(ix) It helps in moulding the attitude of people and it orients them to their environment.

The Process of Communication

A communicator may have some ideas to be conveyed. The ideas have to be encoded and given in the form of a message. Then, a medium is chosen (like written) through which it reaches the receiver. The receiver decodes them and understands the message. He/She is now in a position to react or give a feedback by which the communicator is able to know whether the receiver has understood the message in the way he/she wanted it to be.

A manager in a company has the primary responsibility of disseminating the information to the departments, supervisors, clerks and also the other stakeholders outside the company, like the government departments. Each communication has got its own significance and relevance. It is the communication that brings the different departments together. The production department, for example, communicates to the purchase department regarding its requirement of raw material. The marketing department communicates with the Production department regarding the supply of finished products. Likewise, every department interacts with every other department in one way or the other. Even a leave letter needs to be properly worded and communicated. Communication gap may lead to confusion and chaos.

When the communicator wants to send a message, he/she develops the idea in his/her mind and encodes it. Encoding refers to the employment of language in conveying an idea or a message. The language used for encoding must be known to both the communicator and the receiver. Communication may be made through symbols like facial expression, hand and body gestures, groaning, screaming and the like. But by far the most effective means of communication is made through words.

A message may be verbal or non-verbal. Though generally verbal messages are understood more clearly, non-verbal messages may also be useful. In fact, on certain occasions, a non-verbal message may be more effective than a verbal message. For example, during a condolence meeting, speeches will be ineffective. Two minutes of silent prayer will be a better way of showing respect to a departed soul.

The medium chosen for communication is equally important. There are several media by which a message can be communicated; for example, a letter, telephone, or e-mail may be used as a medium of communication. A proper medium is chosen depending upon the situation. Sometimes a letter will be better than a direct talk or vice versa; e-mail is faster than a letter medium but the latter has got its own advantages. An appointment order, for example, is to be made in the letter medium though a message could be sent through e-mail. The advantage of direct spoken medium is that one can add more effectiveness through tonal variations. It can also be a disadvantage. If the tone is harsh, it will reflect anger and spoil the process of communication itself.

In the decoding process, the receiver translates the message into ideas that become meaningful to him/her. The process of decoding will be clearly seen when idiomatic sentences are uttered. For example, when a person says that it is raining cats and dogs, the receiver who knows the idiom understands that it is raining heavily and that cats and dogs have no role in it.

In the process of communication, the receiver is as much important as the sender of the message. Unless the message is correctly understood by the receiver, the communicator's job is not complete. Effective communication is always receiver-oriented but not media-oriented. While communicating a message, the sender will have to bear in mind the level of understanding of the receiver. Only then, the communication will be effective.

Feedback is the end point in a communication process. The feedback is helpful for a communicator in assessing whether the message has been correctly understood by the receiver.

Feedback could be verbal or non-verbal. The receiver may reply to the question of a communicator verbally or he/she (the receiver) may simply nod his head. When a speaker makes a good point, the audience may react positively by clapping their hands or negatively by throwing stones at the speaker. Both are forms of feedback; however the latter, being an aggressive way of responding, is not recommended.

Types of Communication

DOWNWARD AND UPWARD

If the communication flows from the higher official to a lower one, it is called downward communication. In a downward communication, the tone and content will be directive and authoritative. Orders and instructions are conveyed through this type of communication.

On the other hand, an upward communication flows from a lower official to a higher official. Such a communication will generally be in the form of reports, complaints, grievances and the like.

HORIZONTAL AND DIAGONAL COMMUNICATION

A communication between the production department and purchase department is an example of horizontal communication. Such communications are important from the point of view of co-ordination.

In an organization, the sales representatives generally report to the marketing manager and from him/her, the details flow to the other departments like the accounts department.

However, in some occasions, say, for instance, in a situation like financial year-end, the accounts department may seek information directly from the sales representatives. This is known as diagonal communication where the main motive is to save time.

Barriers to Communication

Communication is not always very smooth. There could be a lot of impediments on the way. There could also be certain barriers to communication. Unless the barriers are removed, communication will not be effective. Some of the barriers to the communication are:

SCREENING

The workers in an organization may make a complaint to the manager. The manager is expected to talk to the CEO and try to solve the problem. But, for certain reasons (sometimes personal, sometimes institutional), a manager may edit the words of the workers and present the idea to the CEO in a condensed fashion. While doing so, there is every chance of the message getting distorted.

SELECTION

The workers may give a list of ten complaints to the manager, who in turn may select only a few of them and convey them to the CEO. Hence the complete message does not reach the CEO and, therefore, the communication is incomplete.

EMOTIONS

Emotions are barriers to communication. For example, during an important discussion, the union leaders may provoke a manager. Being stirred up with emotions, if the manager utters some indecent words in a fit of anger, the communication process is marred.

LANGUAGE

Very often, improper or incorrect use of language becomes a barrier to communication. An example will make this clear. When an official retired in a company, a felicitation meeting was organized. One of the speakers wanted to say, "The officer is not only a good administrator but also a good human being." Instead the speaker said, "Only the officer is not a good administrator and only not a good human being also." One can imagine the embarrassment that was created by the speaker's poor use of the language.

Common Barriers to Communication

In addition to those discussed above, there are certain common barriers, particularly to oral communication which must be carefully avoided at all levels. They are:

OVERLOADING OF INFORMATION

Speakers in a seminar often commit such mistakes. In order to convey as much as possible within the given time they load their speech with excessive information, which becomes too heavy for the listener.

DISINTERESTEDNESS

When a visitor at home is speaking, if the listener were to switch on the TV and watch it, the message conveyed by the speaker will not receive proper attention. Disinterestedness on the part of the listener is a barrier to communication in such cases.

SHORTAGE OF TIME

Owing to the shortage of time, some messages may be conveyed in a truncated fashion and so communication gets short-circuited.

Overcoming Barriers

Barriers should not be considered as permanent blocks to progress. Barriers have to be overcome in order to achieve success. In the field of communication also, as in the other fields, barriers have to be broken by positive steps taken in the right direction. They are:

PRIORITIZING

A manager should not get bogged down amidst a heap of messages. There should be an arrangement to pick and choose messages that are very important from the organization's point of view. The principle of management by exception must be followed by him/her. If this is done effectively, the manager can concentrate on decision-making job for which he/she is appointed. Another idea would be to condense and edit the messages that are sent to the manager so that no message is totally omitted.

FEEDBACK

By a proper feedback system, some of the barriers to communication can be broken. On the basis of the feedback, one can refine the language and the content, correct the mistakes and redraft the entire communication. If one medium of communication is found ineffective, another one can be chosen.

SIMPLE LANGUAGE

It is always difficult to make language simple and straight. Many people find it difficult to make a point succinctly. "Brevity is the soul of wit." Therefore, a manager should train himself/herself to convey an idea with fewer words.

LISTENING

Most of the communication barriers can be overcome by simply listening to the views of others. Misunderstanding generally arises only when a person is not given a chance to express himself/herself and or if he/she is not listened to.

CONTROL OF EMOTIONS

Human beings are not machines. They are controlled by feelings or emotions. Though emotions pertain to the mind, they affect every other limb of the body also. We see that when a person becomes emotional, his/her whole body shakes. A person overpowered by emotions speaks in a different tone. In an official circle, there is very little room for emotions. Even when a person is dismissed from service, his/her dismissal order should be politely worded. Control of emotions is necessary in the communication process. In an emotional situation, a manager should desist from taking instant decisions or conveying the message immediately. He/She should postpone the action for some time, regain his/her composure and then start communicating.

ALERTNESS

Before speaking, an administrator should observe the mood of the listeners and plan his/her speech accordingly. Sometimes, the body language or the non-verbal clues of the listeners will be helpful in judging a situation. In an organization, a manager should make use of the informal channels like the union to get the information. The grapevine source could be useful to get an important information during crunch situations. But it is always advisable to depend more on formal channels since information from informal channels are beset with rumors and distorted versions.

Some Guidelines for Reading, Writing and Listening

Books on communication give certain guidelines for the effective use of the medium. They are listed below:

READING

(i) One should read for better understanding.

(ii) Reading should be followed by assimilation of ideas.

(iii) What is read should not remain undigested in the mind.

(iv) The ideas from what one reads should become one's own and be used.

(v) What is read must be shared with others.

(vi) What is read must be used for practical application.

WRITING

(i) One should be precise in writing.

(ii) Writing is different from speaking. Whatever is spoken cannot be put in writing.

(iii) Writing is a mode of commitment and so one should be careful in communicating through the written medium.

(iv) Repetition must be avoided.

(v) Grammatical mistakes may go unnoticed in spoken form. But they will be glaring in written material. One must, therefore, take care to avoid grammatical mistakes.

LISTENING

(i) In speaking, reading and writing, some training can be given. But, for listening, there is very little scope for training. One has to train oneself in listening.

(ii) If one wants to communicate with somebody, one must first understand that person. To understand a person, one must listen to him/her.

(iii) One should listen to others with rapt attention.

(iv) Children and youngsters have to be listened to. Generally parents start instructing them but never listen to them. This is how the generation gap develops.

(v) One should listen to others with a feeling of empathy. Empathic listening is putting oneself in another person's frame of reference. It is not just nodding the head or saying "I agree with you." It is a question of understanding a person fully, deeply and emotionally as well as intellectually.

Essentials of an Efficient Communication

(i) One must carefully plan on what to communicate and how to communicate.

(ii) The objectives must be well defined.

(iii) Audience reaction must be observed.

(iv) Before communication, peers and subordinates may be consulted.

(vi) The medium, the tone and content of the communication must be decided well in advance.

(vii) Time consciousness is necessary.

(viii) The communicator must have the future in mind while communicating.

(viii) Trust and confidence must be created in the minds of the listeners.

(ix) Wherever follow-up work is involved, words must be supported by action.

Some Guidelines for Improving Communication Skill

(i) One should not oversell an idea.

(ii) Efforts for communication should never be given up. Persistence will always pay.

(iii) It is better to use sketches and diagrams to make the communication interesting.

(iv) One should anticipate objections and be well prepared with answers for them.

(v) Communication is a two-way process. One should invite participation from the audience.

(vi) One should give illustrations wherever necessary.

(vii) Speeches may be interspaced with humorous anecdotes.

(viii) One should use suggestive expressions rather than a blunt message.

(ix) One may add one or two riddles here and there to arouse curiosity among the audience.

(x) Effective voice modulation is to be employed to break monotony.

(xi) The body language may be used to good effect.

The Concept of Communication as Developed in Sanskrit Sources

Indian philosophers, logicians, grammarians and rhetoricians approach the problem of communication in a different way. Communication is made through sentences. A sentence consists of words. Words are accompanied by sense. According to Bhartṛhari, the author of *Vākyapadīya*, there exists a permanent relationship between a word and its sense.[6] Just as the sense organs of perception have a natural power to perceive what comes within their purview, so also words have a natural capacity to convey ideas.[7] According to Nyāya and Vaiśeṣika systems, words have a peculiar power called *śakti* which is responsible for conveying a fixed sense. In later Nyāya-Vaiśeṣika texts, this *Śakti* is attributed to God.[8] Kālidāsa says that the word and the sense are united together like Śiva and Pārvatī.[9]

There is a controversy regarding the unit of speech, in Indian systems. According to the logicians, word is the unit of speech. According to one section of the Mīmāṁsakas (Prābhākaras), sentence is the unit of speech. The individual

---

6. नित्यः शब्दार्थसम्बन्धः।
nityaḥ śabdārthasambandhaḥ
— *Vākyapadīya*, I.23

7. इन्द्रियाणां स्वविषयेष्वनादिर्योग्यता यथा।
अनादिरर्थैः शब्दानां सम्बन्धो योग्यता तथा।।
indriyāṇāṁ svaviṣayeṣvanādiryogyatā yathā ।
anādirarthaiḥ śabdānāṁ sambandho yogyatā tathā ।।
— Ibid., III.3.29

8. अस्मात् पदात् अयमर्थो बोद्धव्य
इति ईश्वरसंकेतः शक्तिः।
asmāt padāt ayamartho boddhavya
iti īśvarasaṁketaḥ śaktiḥ ।।
— *Tarkasaṁgraha*, 8.1

see also *Siddhāntamuktāvalī* (Ed. KSS, Benaras 1951) p. 265:

शक्तिश्च पदेन सह पदार्थस्य सम्बन्धः।
śaktiśca padena saha padārthasya sambandhaḥ ।

9. वागर्थाविव संपृक्तौ वागर्थप्रतिपत्तये।
जगतः पितरौ वन्दे पार्वतीपरमेश्वरौ।।
vāgarthāviva saṁpṛktau vāgarthapratipattaye ।
jagataḥ pitarau vande pārvatīparameśvarau ।।
— *Raghuvaṁśa*, I.1

words do not convey any meaning except in the context of a sentence.

Rhetoricians speak of threefold power of words, *abhidhā*, *lakṣaṇā* and *vyañjanā*.[10]

ABHIDHĀ

Abhidhā refers to the primary meaning of a word. There are different ways by which we learn the meanings of words.

(i) ***Usage of words by elders***: For example, "A" utters the sentence "Open the door." "B" does the action conveyed by the sentence; and "C" keeps observing. Then "A" utters "Open the window" and "B" does the action. By comparing both the sentences and by observing the common action of "Opening" "C" comes to know what door and window mean.

(ii) ***Through direct statement of a trustworthy authority***: For example, the child learns words and their meanings from its parents.

(iii) ***Grammar***: We learn the meanings of roots, suffixes and derivatives from grammar.

In fact, the most important use of grammar is to help one to learn a language quickly and correctly.

(iv) ***Analogy***: We see from our experience that if a general rule is taught with the help of one example, similar examples can be given on the basis of analogy. For example, a teacher would teach that to form plural, one must add "s" to the singular form. If "boy" becomes "boys" in plural, "girl" becomes "girls." Then the grammar takes care of the exceptions.

---

10. For a fuller treatment of these concepts, see K. Kunjunni Raja, *Indian Theories of meaning*.

(v) ***Lexicon***: Lexicons and dictionaries are helpful in knowing the meanings of words in a new language through a known language.

(vi) ***Explanation***: Language does not remain constant, it keeps changing. We are not able to understand the meanings of some of the words used in old literature. In such cases, the commentary of the work comes to our help.

(vii) ***Syntactic connection with words already known***: The meaning of a new word is sometimes learnt by its relation to other words in a sentence that are already known. In a sentence, "Bharatanāṭyam is an excellent form of Indian dance," the meaning of the word "Bharatanāṭyam" is understood with the help of other words in the sentence that are already known.

(viii) ***Contextual factor***: Some words may have two or more meanings. The exact sense of its use is understood in relation to the context in which it is uttered. For example, in Sanskrit, the word *saindhava* has two meanings, namely, salt and a horse. When the word is uttered while mixing the curd rice it means salt. If uttered by a warrior ready to go to the battlefield, it refers to the horse.

LAKṢAṆĀ

Lakṣaṇā may be translated as metaphorical extension. Sometimes a word is used to denote a referent other than its normal use. If we take the primary meaning, the sentence may become nonsensical in the context. When a person says, "My office is on the Mount Road" it does not mean that his office is at the centre of the road obstructing the traffic. In order to emphasize the proximity, the speaker has used a metaphor. Some more examples can be given to explain the nature of *lakṣaṇā*:

(i) ***Association:*** In the sentence, "The rifles are entering the camp," "rifles" means soldiers carrying the rifles. The association of rifle and the soldier is responsible for the usage.

(ii) ***Location:*** In the sentence, "The cots are crying" for example, the word "cots" refers to babies. In this sentence, reference to location is important.

(iii) ***Behaviour:*** In the sentence, "The manager is killing me," the speaker refers to the volume of work dumped on him/her by the manager. The "behaviour" comes into play here.

(iv) ***Measure:*** The phrase "one litre" uttered in a milk vendor's shop refers to the measure.

(v) ***Quality:*** When one says "I love that beauty," he/she refers to the quality of the object.

(vi) ***Livelihood:*** In the sentence "Music is life for me," the cause of livelihood is referred.

(vii) ***Prominence:*** In the sentence, "He is the Government," the sense of "prominence" is intended.

(viii) ***Similarity:*** In the sentence "He is lion-hearted," similarity comes into play.

(ix) ***Irony:*** In the sentence, "He thinks that he is Einstein," irony is meant.

VYAÑJANĀ

Vyañjanā may be translated as suggestion. It is a matter of common experience that an utterance may mean much more than literal sense. Even in metaphorical sentences like, "The pistols are entering the camp," the literal sense becomes secondary. There is another type of sentence where neither the literal meaning nor a metaphor will be having any significance; in fact, the metaphor may be absent there. Some other special meaning may flash in the mind of a discerning reader. It will be suggested and such a meaning will shine more prominently than the literal meaning. An example will make this clear:

सुवर्णपुष्पां पृथिवीं छिन्वन्ति पुरुषास्त्रयः।
शूरश्च कृतविद्यश्च यश्च जानाति सेवितुम्।।

suvarṇapuṣpāṁ pṛthivīṁ chinvanti puruṣāstrayaḥ।
śūraśca kṛtavidyaśca yaśca jānāti sevitum।।

Three types of men reap a harvest of golden flowers on earth. They are, a heroic man, a learned man and a man who knows how to serve others (and get benefits for himself).[11]

Here, the expression "harvesting the golden flowers" does not fit in since there is nothing like a golden flower that can be grown or harvested. It only means "prosperity." (If a person were to grow and harvest golden flowers, he will indeed be prosperous.) So, the primary meaning is dropped here and we take the suggested sense, that is, "prosperity." A figure of speech like the simile is already beautiful. If it is suggested, instead of being explicitly stated, it can be all the more charming. As for an emotion, it can never be stated in so many words. It can only be suggested. If a person simply utters the word "joke," nobody will laugh. But if he/she describes a humorous situation, people will laugh. The sentence uttered by him/her should contain humour in it. When a person says "My village is on the Ganges," the metaphorical sense is that it is very close to the Ganges. Going further "the coolness," "purity" and "sanctity" of being close to the Ganges are suggested.

11. See *Dhvanyāloka* (ed. K. Krishnamurthy, Karnataka University, 1974), p. 28.

Sanskrit grammarians and philosophers discuss the syntactic unity of a sentence. They speak of four factors that bring about syntactic unity of a sentence. The first one is called *ākāṅkṣa* or mutual expectancy of words. For example, a verb like "bring" has expectancy for a word denoting some object like "book." Similarly, the word "book" expects the verb "bring." The next one is *yogyatā* or compatibility. For example, the sentence "he wets it with water" has compatibility but not the sentence "he wets it with fire" since fire can only burn but not make anything wet. The third one is *āsatti* which is explained as the condition that the words in a sentence should be contiguous in time. For example, if a person utters the word "close" today and "the door" tomorrow, the contiguity is lost and the sense will not be conveyed.

The last one is called *tātparya* or the meaning intended by the speaker. A sentence like "The sun has set" may mean several things to several people. A religious person may think that it is time for him/her to go to the temple. For a mother, it is time for the children to stop playing and start studying. For an employee in an office, it is time to close the files and leave the office. For a harlot, it is time to welcome her customers. For a thief, it is time to start the business. But the speaker would have simply meant that it was time to wind up his/her evening walk. This is the meaning intended by the speaker.

Marks of a Good Communication According to the Arthaśāstra

The *Arthaśāstra* gives a list of six important factors that contribute to good communication skill:

अर्थक्रमः संबन्धः परिपूर्णता माधुर्यमौदार्यं
स्पष्टत्वमिति लेखसंपत्।

arthakramaḥ saṁbandhaḥ paripūrṇatā mādhuryamaudāryaṁ spaṣṭatvamiti lekhasaṁpat ।

— *Arthaśāstra*, 2.10.6

They are: *arthakrama, sambandha, paripūrṇatā, mādhurya, audārya* and *spaṣṭatva*. All these tally with the principles of communication as dealt within management books.

ARTHAKRAMA

Arthakrama refers to the arrangement of the subject matter. In a communication, attention should be paid to priorities, that is, what should be stated first, what should follow and in what order. There should be cogency with respect to the order of things that are stated. For example, if a mission is taken up, the draft resolution should state the objectives, the necessity of the mission, the possibility of a solution, the conditions for carrying out the objectives and the pros and cons of the mission.

For example, during his peace mission, Kṛṣṇa presents all these in his speech.[12]

(i) The purpose of his visit, (ii) root cause of the war, (iii) why peace is advocated, (iv) the possibility of peace, (v) who should take decision on peace, (vi) conditions for peace (vii) his qualifications as a peacemaker, (viii) how peace can be made, and (ix) what will happen if peace proposal is rejected. On the purpose of his visit, Kṛṣṇa says, "I have come here to propose peace between Kauravas and Pāṇḍavas, so that destruction of warriors on either side could be prevented." Then Kṛṣṇa states the cause of the war: "Dhṛtarāṣṭra, these sons of yours, headed by Duryodhana, are behaving like wicked men pushing behind nobility and material good." Then peace is advocated, since there will be large-scale destruction

12. *The Mahābhārata*, Udyoga Parva, 95.3ff.

in the case of a war between the two sides. For Kauravas, it will be a total destruction. Peace is possible even at this stage. The onus is now on Dhṛtarāṣṭra since Kṛṣṇa himself would sign the treaty on behalf of the Pāṇḍavas if the peace proposal is accepted. The condition for peace is that the Pāṇḍavas should be given their due share of the kingdom.

SAṀBANDHA

Saṁbandha is the statement of subject matter with complete compatibility between the parts of the statement. There should be no ambiguity in the statement. An example can be given.

त्यजेत् कुलार्थे पुरुषं ग्रामस्यार्थे कुलं त्यजेत् ।
ग्रामं जनपदस्यार्थे आत्मार्थे पृथिवीं त्यजेत् ॥

tyajet kulārthe puruṣaṁ grāmasyārthe kulaṁ tyajet ।
grāṁa janapadasyārthe ātmārthe pṛthivīṁ tyajet ॥
— *Mahābhārata*, Udyoga Parva, 37.15

An individual may be abandoned for the sake of the family, a family for the sake of a village, a village for the sake of the country; and the whole earth for sake of realizing one's own soul.

PARIPŪRṆATĀ

Paripūrṇatā or completeness results when a statement is self-explanatory with reason, illustration and the like. An example can be given from Kālidāsa's *Abhijñānaśākuntalam*. Duṣyanta, who is captivated by Śakuntalā's beauty has a doubt whether she would be given away in marriage at all. If she is supposed to remain as a life-long ascetic, his hopes would be dashed to pieces. Meanwhile Śakuntalā's friends make it clear that Śakuntalā is only the foster daughter of sage Kaṇva who is looking for a suitable husband for her. Duṣyanta says:

भव हृदय साभिलाषं सम्प्रति संदेह निर्णयो जातः।
आशङ्कसे यदग्निं तदिदं स्पर्शक्षमं रत्नम्॥

bhava hṛdaya sābhilāṣaṁ samprati saṅdeha nirṇayo jātaḥ।
āśaṅkase yadagniṁ tadidaṁ sparśākṣamaṁ ratnam॥

— *Abhijñānaśākuntalam*, I.28

O, heart, be hopeful (statement) for now all doubts are cleared (reason). What you thought to be fire, is a gem capable of being touched (Illustration).

MĀDHURYA

Mādhurya is the use of words that have a pleasing sense. The *Mahābhārata* says that the following give delight:

समागमश्च सखिभिः महांश्चैव धनागमः।
पुत्रेण च परिष्वङ्गः सन्निपातश्च मैथुने॥
समये च प्रियालापः सयूथेषु समुन्नतिः॥

samāgamaśca sakhībhiḥ mahāṁścaiva dhanāgamaḥ।
putreṇa ca pariṣvaṅgaḥ sannipātaśca maithune॥
samaye ca priyālāpaḥ sayūtheṣu samunnatiḥ॥

— *Udyoga*, I.104

Union with friends, acquisition of wealth, embrace of a son, conjugal love, sweet conversation at an appropriate time, elevation in one's own community — these contribute to delight.

AUDĀRYA

Audārya is exaltedness. It is the representation of noble ideas through decent expression. For example:

नास्ति विद्यासमं चक्षुः नास्ति सत्यसमं तपः।
नास्ति रागसमं दुःखं नास्ति त्यागसमं सुखम्॥

nāsti vidyāsamaṁ cakṣuḥ nāsti satyasamaṁ tapaḥ।
nāsti rāgasamaṁ duḥkhaṁ nāsti tyāgasamaṁ sukhaṁ.
— *Mahābhārata,* Śānti Parva, 183.4-5

There is no eye equal to learning, no penance equal to the observance of truth, no misery equal to desire and no happiness equal to renunciation.

SPAṢṬATVA

Spaṣṭatva is clarity of expression. In order to ensure clarity of expression one must avoid obsolete words and pompous language. Johnsonian expressions like "His stance changed from perpendicularity to horizontality" (meaning simply, he fell down) may be avoided. A report in an office said, "The machine has a tendency to develop excessive and unpleasant audile symptoms when operating at elevated temperature." The sentence can very will be rendered as "The machine tends to get noisy when it runs hot."

The famous *Rāmāyaṇa* stanza can be quoted as an instance of clarity of expression.

सत्यं ब्रूयात् प्रियं ब्रूयात् न ब्रूयात् सत्यमप्रियम्।
प्रियं च नानृतं ब्रूयात् एष धर्मः सनातनः॥

satyaṁ brūyāt priyaṁ brūyāt na brūyāt satyam apriyam।
priyaṁ ca na anṛtaṁ brūyāt eṣa dharmaḥ sanātanaḥ॥[13]

Truth must be uttered; it should be pleasing as well. Do not speak the truth that may cause unpleasantness. At the same time, do not speak falsehood that may be pleasing. This is the eternal virtue.

The *Mahābhārata* makes a valid point on good speech. It says:

13. Quoted in V. Gopala Iyengar's First Book of Sanskrit, verse no. 105.

अभ्यावहति कल्याणं विविधं वाक् सुभाषिता।
सैव दुर्भाषिता राजन्ननर्थायोपपद्यते॥

abhyāvahati kalyāṇaṁ vividhaṁ vāk subhāṣitā।
saiva durbhāṣitā rājannanarthāyopapadyate॥

— *Vidura-Nīti*, II.78

A speech, well spoken, brings in various kinds of benefits while the same, if ill spoken, tends to create troubles.

It further says:

रोहते सायकैर्विद्धं वने पशुना हतम्।
वाचा दुरुक्तंबीभत्सं न संरोहति वाक्क्षतम्॥
rohate sāyakairviddhaṁ vane paśunā hatam।
v ācā duruktaṁ bibhatsaṁ na saṁrohati vākkṣatam॥

— Ibid., II.79

The wounds caused by arrows get healed in due course. Likewise, a forest, cut down by axe, sprouts again. But a verbal wound caused by words, ill spoken, will never be healed.

A similar idea is expressed in the *Tirukkuraḷ* also:

A wound caused by burns will get healed, bot not the one caused by the tongue (words)

— *Tirukkuraḷ*, 129

The time of utterance is very important in a communication. The *Mahābhārata* says:

अप्राप्तकालं वचनं बृहस्पतिरपि ब्रुवन्।
लभते बुद्ध्यवज्ञानमवमानं च भारत॥

aprāptakālaṁ vacanaṁ bṛhaspatirapi bruvan।
labhate buddhyavajñānamavamānaṁ ca bhārata॥

— *Vidura-Nīti*, VII.2

Even Bṛhaspati (the God of speech) will incur rebuke and disrespect if he were to speak something not befitting the time (occasion).

In the communication process, the receiver is as much important as the sender of the message. The *Mahābhārata* gives guidelines for a good listener.

क्षिप्रं विजानाति चिरं शृणोति
विज्ञाय चार्थं भजते न कामात्।
नासंपृष्टो व्यपयुङ्क्ते परार्थे
तत् प्रज्ञानं प्रथमं पण्डितस्य।।

kṣipraṁ vijānāti ciraṁ śṛṇoti
vijñāya cārthaṁ bhajate na kāmāt ।
nāsaṁpṛṣṭo vyapayuṅkte parārthe
tat prajñānaṁ prathamaṁ paṇḍitasya ।।

— Ibid., I.29

The listener should listen for long but quickly grasp what is spoken. He must apply the principles learnt, dispassionately. Unasked, he should not preach others. This is the mark of a learned man.

The *Mahābhārata* gives some clues for a good communicator:

प्रवृत्तवाक् चित्रकथ ऊहवान् प्रतिभानवान्।
आशु ग्रन्थस्य वक्ता च यस्स पण्डित उच्यते।।

pravṛttavāk citrakatha ūhavān pratibhānavān ।
āśu granthasya vaktā ca yassa paṇḍita ucyate ।।

— Ibid., I.35

He who speaks boldly, discourses eloquently on diverse topics in an inspiring manner, sees the pros and cons of everything, is endowed with a ready insight into every problem that arises, quotes texts spontaneously and interprets them intelligently.

Official Communique

As to what can be communicated in an official document, the *Arthaśāstra* says:

निन्दा प्रशंसा पृच्छा च तथाख्यानमथार्थना।
प्रत्याख्यानमुपालम्भः प्रतिषेधोऽथ चोदना।।
सान्त्वमभ्युपपत्तिश्च भर्त्सनानुनयौ तथा।
एतेष्वर्थाः प्रवर्तन्ते त्रयोदशसु लेखजाः।।

nindā praśaṁsā pṛcchā ca tathākhyānamathārthanā।
pratyākhyānamupālambhaḥ pratiṣedho 'tha codanā।।
sāntvamabhyupapattiśca bhartsanānunayau tathā।
eteṣvarthāḥ pravartante trayodaśasu lekhajāḥ।।

— *Arthaśāstra*, 2.10.23-24

Censure, praise, query, statement of facts, request, refusal, pointing out the mistake, prohibition, injunction, appeasement, help, threat and happiness.

Censure may be used to pull up the subordinates if they have committed a mistake, but it should be expressed politely.

For example, when Arjuna stands perplexed in the battle front, Kṛṣṇa censures him, but in a dignified way without causing any damage to Arjuna's reputation as a great warrior.

कुतस्त्वा कश्मलमिदं विषमे समुपस्थितम्।
अनार्यजुष्टमस्वर्ग्यमकीर्तिकरमर्जुन।।

kutastvā kaśmalamidaṁ viṣame samupasthitam।
anāryajuṣṭamasvargyamakīrtikaramarjuna।।

— *Bhagavad-Gītā*, II.2

How has this confusion overtaken you at this critical juncture? It is unbecoming of a noble soul, it will not lead to heaven and it will not contribute to your fame.

When a person deserves appreciation, he/she must be praised, but it should be spontaneous. A Sanskrit *subhāṣita* gives a guideline on who should be praised and when.

प्रत्यक्षे गुरवः स्तुत्याः परोक्षे मित्रबान्धवाः।
कर्मान्ते दासभृत्याश्च पुत्रा नैव तथा स्त्रियः॥

pratyakṣe guravaḥ stutyāḥ parokṣe mitrabāndhavāḥ ।
karmānte dāsabhṛtyāśca putrā naiva tathā striyaḥ ॥
— *Su*, p. 159, verse 273

The teachers and elders should be praised in their presence. Friends and relatives may be praised in their absence. But one's own children should never be praised at all.

The idea is that the children can be encouraged but they should not be praised openly. Otherwise, overconfidence and complacency may set in impeding their progress. Praise should come from the heart and it should not simply be an outward expression of words alone. Such a praise will only amount to flattery. Duṣyanta, being fascinated by the natural beauty of Śakuntalā praises her thus:

सरसिजमनुविद्धं शैवलेनापि रम्यं
मलिनमपि हिमांशोर्लक्ष्म लक्ष्मीं तनोति।
इयमधिकमनोज्ञा वल्कलेनापि तन्वी
किमिव हि मधुराणां मण्डनं नाकृतीनाम्॥

sarasijamanuviddhaṁ śaivalenāpi ramyaṁ
malinamapi himāṁśorlakṣma lakṣmīṁ tanoti ।
iyamadhikamanojñā valkalenāpi tanvī
kimiva hi madhurāṇāṁ maṇḍanaṁ nākṛtīnām ॥
— *Abhijñānaśākuntalam*, I.20

Though covered by the moss, yet the lotus looks beautiful. Though having a black spot in it, the moon looks beautiful. Though wearing only bark garments, this girl looks very beautiful. What does not add to the charm of naturally beautiful people?

As for a query, the entire *kaccit sarga* of the *Rāmāyaṇa* is an excellent example. A similar *kaccit sarga* is available in the *Mahābhārata* also (Sabhā-Parva) where Nārada enquires Yudhiṣṭhira about his administration:

> कच्चित्कृतं विजानीषे कर्तारं न प्रशंससि।
> सतां मध्ये महाराज सत्करोषि च पूजनम्।।
>
> *kaccitkr̥taṁ vijānīṣe kartāraṁ na praśaṁsasi* ।
> *satāṁ madhye mahārāja satkaroṣi ca pūjanam* ।।
> — *Mahābhārata*, Sabhā Parva, C. p. 100

> O king, do you recognize a work done, acclaim the doer and honour him with rewards in the midst of good people?

In this verse, we also get an idea about motivation. Recognition of merit is one of the important factors for motivation. According to Maslow's theory of organizational behaviour, human needs are classified thus into five levels in hierarchical fashion.

1. Physiological needs
2. Safety and security
3. Belongingness
4. Self-esteem
5. Self-actualization

The physiological needs can be satisfied through economic factors and that is why the adequate reward for the work done is recommended. The safety and security needs arise from the instincts of self-preservation and a concern for the future. A sense of belongingness can be infused into the minds of subordinates by establishing a warm, harmonious inter-personal relationship. Everybody feels that his/her work, capability and strength must be recognized and appreciated. Frustration causes an inferiority complex, a state of weakness and helplessness. In order to avoid such feelings among the subordinates, an administrator has to acclaim the merits of the good workers in public and acknowledge their contribution. Self-actualization is the desire to become what one is capable of becoming. This can be done by enthusing the subordinates to set higher goals for themselves and to achieve them. All these ideas are briefly stated in the *Mahābhārata* verse cited.

A request will be entertained only if it is convincing and so a communication containing a request should be properly worded. An expression of humility in the request may generally ensure its acceptance. We make a request to somebody only when we find it impossible to achieve an object by ourselves. A manager is not one who does things himself/herself; he/she should get the work done through others. While doing so, a request may be more effective than a command. While seeking knowledge, request alone would work. For example, Arjuna makes this humble request to Kṛṣṇa:

कार्पण्यदोषोपहतस्वभावः
पृच्छामि त्वां धर्मसंमूढचेताः।
यच्छ्रेयः स्यान्निश्चितं ब्रूहि तन्मे
शिष्यस्तेऽहं शाधि मां त्वां प्रपन्नम्॥

kārpaṇyadoṣopahatasvabhāvaḥ
pṛcchāmi tvāṁ dharmasaṁmūḍacetāḥ ।
yacchreyaḥ syānniścitaṁ brūhi tanme
śiṣyaste 'haṁ śādhi māṁ tvāṁ prapannam ॥
— *Bhagavad-Gītā*, II.7

With my normal nature being spoiled by weakness and with my mind confused about what exactly my duty is, I am asking you. Please instruct what is proper for me. I am your disciple. Please save me. I surrender unto you.

A statement of facts has to be precise. An example can be given from the *Abhijñānaśākuntalam.*

Duṣyanta and Śakuntalā are married secretly. By the quirk of fate, Duṣyanta who had returned to his capital forgets the entire episode. Śakuntalā becomes pregnant. Sage Kaṇva who returns from pilgrimage after a few months comes to know of the entire episode. He arranges to send his daughter to her husband's place with the following message:

त्वमर्हतां प्राग्रसरः स्मृतोऽसि नः
शकुन्तला मूर्तिमती च सत्क्रिया।
समानयंस्तुल्यगुणं वधूवरं
चिरस्य वाच्यं न गतः प्रजापतिः॥

tvamarhatāṁ prāgrasaraḥ smṛto 'si naḥ
śakuntalā mūrtimatī ca satkriyā।
samānayaṁstulyaguṇaṁ vadhūvaraṁ
cirasya vācyaṁ na gataḥ prajāpatiḥ॥

— *Abhijñānaśākuntalam,* V.15

By reciprocal agreement you have married this daughter of mine. I have approved the marriage with pleasure.

You are the best among worthy men. Śakuntalā is virtue in human form. The creator has united a bride and bridegroom of equal merit after a long time, thus escaping from censure.

When it is impossible to comply with a request or an order, a "refusal" is conveyed to the person concerned. Generally, it is a frank or even a blunt statement but, in a good communication, even a refusal is expressed in a polite manner. For example, when Arjuna stands perplexed in the battle front, Kṛṣṇa asks him to carry on with his job of destroying the enemies. But Arjuna conveys his refusal politely:

गुरूनहत्वा हि महानुभावान्
श्रेयो भोक्तुं भैक्ष्यमपीह लोके।
हत्वार्थकामांस्तु गुरूनिहैव
भुञ्जीय भोगान् रुधिरप्रदिग्धान्।।5।।

gurūnahatvā hi mahānubhāvān
śreyo bhoktuṁ bhaikṣyamapīha loke।
hatvārthakāmāṁstu gurūnihaiva
bhuñjīya bhogān rudhirapradigdhān।।5।।

न हि प्रपश्यामि ममापनुद्याद्
यच्छोकमुच्छोषणमिन्द्रियाणाम्।
अवाप्य भूमावसपत्नमृद्धं
राज्यं सुराणामपि चाधिपत्यम्।।8।।

na hi prapaśyāmi mamāpanudyād
yacchokamucchoṣaṇamindriyāṇām।
avāpya bhūmāvasapatnamṛddhaṁ
rājyaṁ surāṇāmapi cādhipatyam।।8।।

संजय उवाच -
एवमुक्त्वा हृषीकेशं गुडाकेशः परंतप।
न योत्स्य इति गोविन्दमुक्त्वा तूष्णीं बभूव ह।।9।।

Sañjaya uvāca —
evamuktvā hṛṣīkeśaṁ guḍākeśaḥ parantapa।
na yotsya iti govindamuktvā tūṣṇīṁ babhūva ha।।9।।
— *Bhagavad-Gītā*, II.5,8-9

It is better to live on alms in this world without killing these noble elders, because even after killing them, we will enjoy only blood-stained pleasures in the form of wealth and sense enjoyment.

For, even on obtaining undisputed sovereignty and an affluent kingdom on this earth, I do not see any means that can drive away the grief, which is drying up my sense.

Having thus spoken to Kṛṣṇa, Arjuna again told him that he would not fight and kept quiet.

Upālambha means "blaming" or "pointing out the mistake." When there are mistakes, they have to be pointed out, but it should not look like blaming somebody unnecessarily or finding a scapegoat nor should it sound like an insult.

When the king refuses to accept Śakuntalā, the helpless girl cries bitterly. At this juncture, the hermit who accompanied her (Śārṅgarava) says:

अतः परीक्ष्य कर्तव्यं विशेषात्संगतं रहः।
अज्ञातहृदयेष्वेवं वैरीभवति सौहृदम्॥

ataḥ parīkṣya kartavyaṁ viśeṣātsaṁgataṁ rahaḥ।
ajñātahṛdayeṣvevaṁ vairībhavati sauhṛdam।

— *Abhijñānaśākuntalam*, V.24

Therefore, a union, especially a secret one ought to be formed with great circumspection; with those who know not each other's heart, love thus turns into hate.

The hermit blames both the king and Śakuntalā for the turn of events, without insulting them.

In the prohibition of an act, the reasoning has to be powerful and the logic unassailable. This in what we find in Gāndhārī's words when she prohibits gambling:

मा कुलस्य क्षरे घोरे कारणं त्वं भविष्यसि।
बद्धं सेतुं को नु भिन्द्याद् धर्मेच्छान्न च पावकम्॥

mā kulasya kṣare ghore kāraṇaṁ tvaṁ bhaviṣyasi।
baddhaṁ setuṁ ko nu bhindyād dharmecchānna ca pāvakam॥

— *Mahābhārata*, Sabhā Parva, C. p. 153

Do not become the cause of the terrible destruction of our

family; who will break the dam that has been built? Who will kindle the extinguished fire? Who will insult the Pāṇḍavas that have settled for peace?

Who will infuriate the Pāṇḍavas who have settled for peace? O, king, on my word, let this disgrace of the family, Duryodhana, be abandoned.

It is a pity that Gāndhārī's words were not heeded and this resulted in the destruction of the Kauravas.

An injunction has to be firm and authoritative. We have an example in the *Mahābhārata*:

Affectionate words, pleasing to the ears of all beings must be spoken; reviling, scandal and violence in language are forbidden; insulting others, egotism andhypocrisy are condemned.

वत्सलस्सर्वभूतानां वाच्याः श्रोत्रसुखा गिरः।
परिवादापवादौ च पारुष्यं चात्र गर्हितम्॥
अवज्ञानमहंकारो दम्भश्चैव विगर्हितः॥

vatsalassarvabhūtānāṁ vācyāḥ śrotrasukhā giraḥ।
parivādāpavādau ca pāruṣyaṁ cātra garhitam॥
avajñānamahaṁkāro dambhaścaiva vigarhitaḥ॥
— *Mahābhārata*, Sabhā Parva, C. p. 410

Difference of opinion and misunderstanding are bound to occur between individuals. But an administrator must try to appease the affected party through a proper communication. While living in the forest, Draupadī becomes impatient and blames the Creator of partiality, citing their own calamity and the prosperity of the Kauravas. For this, Yudhiṣṭhira says:

धर्म एव प्लवो नान्यत्स्वर्गं द्रौपदि गच्छताम्।
ईश्वरं चापि भूतानां धातारं मा च वै क्षिप॥

dharma eva plavo nānyatsvargaṁ draupadi gacchatām।
īśvaraṁ cāpi bhūtānāṁ dhātāraṁ mā ca vai kṣipa।।
— *Mahābhārata,* Sabhā Prava, C. p. 169

Princess, I do not observe *dharma* expecting fruit out of it. But my very nature and mind are set on *dharma* only. He who exploits *dharma* misses its true purpose.

Dharma alone is the boat for those who want to go to heaven. Do not blame the Lord who is the creator of all beings.

Help can be procured even from unfriendly camps through communicating skills. There are many such political manoeuvres in the play *Mudrārākṣasa* of Viśākhadatta.

A certain amount of threat may be needed for a leader to bring about discipline. This is what Kṛṣṇa adopts when he senses that his peace mission may fail. He threatens Duryodhana of grave consequences:

यच्चेभ्यो याचमानेभ्य: पित्र्यंशं न दित्यसि।
तच्च पाप प्रदाताऽसि भ्रष्टैश्वर्यो निपातित:।।

yaccebhyo yācamānebhyaḥ pitṛyaṁśaṁ na dityasi।
tacca pāpa pradātā 'si bhraṣṭaiśvaryo nipātitaḥ।।
— *Mahābhārata,* Sabhā Parva, C. p. 268

That which you do not like to give to the Pāṇḍavas who beg for their rightful paternal share, will be taken away forcibly from you and you will fall from your grace and power.

In propitiation, there should be an expression of sincerity and devotion. When Draupadī's appeal to the elders of the court and to her own husbands failed to save her, she propitiated Lord Kṛṣṇa and appealed to him fervently. Then came help from the Lord.

शङ्खचक्रगदापाणे द्वारकानिलयाच्युत।
गोविन्द पुण्डरीकाक्ष रक्ष मां शरणागतम्।।

śaṁkhacakragadāpāṇe dvārakānilayācyuta ।
govinda puṇḍarīkākṣa rakṣa māṁ śaraṇāgatam ।।
— *Mahābhārata*, Sabhā Parva, C. p. 138

O Lord, armed with conch, discus, and mace, O, the lotus-eyed Govinda, protect me who has sought refuge in You. O, Kṛṣṇa, where are you? Why do you neglect the helpless person who is in a crisis.

Kṛṣṇa, the great *yogin*, the Soul of the Universe, the creator of the Universe, Govinda, save the suppliant creature perishing in the midst of the Kurus.

If the propitiation is sincere enough, the appeal connected with it will definitely be answered and so is the case with respect to Draupadī. She is saved by the Lord at the right moment.

Communication will be effective if it is made spicy with a tinge of humour. This verse from the *Mahābhārata* has humour and satire in it:

अनर्थे चैव निरतमर्थे चैव पराङ्मुखम्।
न तं भर्तारमिच्छन्ति षण्डं पतिमिव स्त्रियः।।

anarthe caiva niratamarthe caiva parāṅmukham ।
na taṁ bhartāramicchanti ṣaṇḍaṁ patimiva striyaḥ ।।
— *Vidura-Nīti*, II.21

People do not like to have him as their ruler who is ever intent on useless pursuits and averse to the useful ones, like women who would not like to have the eunuchs as their husbands.

Truth is the very essence of communication, but raw truth may sometimes do more harm than good. So the *Mahābhārata* says:

तस्माद्वक्ष्यामि ते राजन् हितं यत् स्यात् कुरून् प्रति।
वचः श्रेयस्करं धर्म्यं ब्रुवतस्तन्निबोध मे।।

tasmādvakṣyāmi te rājan hitaṁ yat syāt kurūn prati ।
vacaḥ śreyaskaraṁ dharmyaṁ bruvatastannibodha me ॥

— Ibid., II.5

Truth is to be uttered but it has to be pleasant. Do not speak that truth that brings about harm. A falsehood though pleasant should not be spoken.

If the communication is in the form of an advice, the *Mahābhārata* gives the following guidelines:

शुभं वा यदि वा पापं द्वेष्यं वा यदि वा प्रियम्।
नापृष्टः कस्यचिद्ब्रूयाद्यस्य नेच्छेत् पराभवम्॥

śubhaṁ vā yadi vā pāpaṁ dveṣyaṁ vā yadi vā priyaṁ ।
nāpṛṣṭaḥ kasyacidbrūyādyasya necchet parābhavam ॥

— Ibid., II.4

Unasked, one should not advise, whether good or bad, agreeable or not, lest one should wish to incur disrespect.

An administrator should be careful about his communication. He should not blame others unnecessarily. The *Mahābhārata* says:

परं क्षिपति दोषेण वर्तमानः स्वयं तथा।
यश्च क्रुद्ध्यत्यनीशानः स च मूढतमो नरः॥

paraṁ kṣipati doṣeṇa vartamānaḥ svayaṁ tathā ।
yaśca kruddhyatyanīśānaḥ sa ca mūḍhatamo naraḥ ॥

— Ibid., I.45

A good administrator should be aware of his own limitations and mistakes. That man who is himself blameful yet casts blame on others over whom he has no mastery, is a bad administrator.

There should be an element of suspense in the communication. It will create an interest in the minds of the listeners and arouse their curiosity. A verse from the *Mahābhārata* can be cited in this context:

एकया द्वे विनिश्चित्य त्रींश्चतुर्भिर्वशे कुरु।
पञ्च जित्वा विदित्वा षट् सप्त हित्वा सुखी भव॥

ekayā dve viniścitya trīṁścaturbhirvarśe kuru ।
pañca jitvā viditvā ṣaṭ sapta hitvā sukhī bhava ॥
— Ibid., I.51

By one, discriminate two, control three by four. Conquering five, knowing six and giving up seven, be happy (one — intellect; two — right and the wrong; three — friend, foe, neutral; four — conciliation, use of money, divisive tactics, punishment; five — the five senses; six — the six measures of foreign policy; seven — the seven vices, namely women, wine, gambling, hunting, harsh words, severity of punishment and waste of wealth).

Harshness should be avoided in a communication. The *Mahābhārata* says:

द्वे कर्मणी नरः कुर्वन्नस्मिन् लोके विरोचते।
अब्रुवन् परुषं किञ्चिदसतो नार्चयंस्तथा॥

dve karmaṇī naraḥ kurvannasmin loke virocate ।
abruvan paruṣaṁ kiñcidasato nārcayaṁstathā ॥
— Ibid., I.61

By not speaking harsh words and by not worshipping the wicked, a man becomes famous.

A proper control is necessary in the use of words. We have a reference in *Vidura-Nīti*:

वाक्संयमो हि नृपते सुदुष्करतमो मतः।
अर्थवच्च विचित्रं च न शक्यं बहु भाषितुम्॥

vāksaṁyamo hi nṛpate suduṣkaratamo mataḥ ।
arthavacca vicitraṁ ca na śakyaṁ bahu bhāṣitūm ॥

— Ibid., II.77

Control of speech is said to be the most difficult one and to hold on a long discourse with elegance and substance is not easy too.

Communication is a two-way process. The receiver will have to respond effectively for the communication process to be completed. This response should be positive. Evasive answers or a weak reply (not to the point) will lead nowhere. The *Mahābhārata* says:

पृष्टो धर्मं न विब्रूयात् गोकर्णशिथिलं चरन्।
धर्माद्भ्रश्यति राजंस्तु नास्य लोकोऽस्ति न प्रजा॥

pṛṣṭo dharmaṁ na vibrūyāt gokarṇaśithilaṁ caran ।
dharmādbhraśyati rājaṁstu nāsya loko 'sti na prajāḥ ॥

— Ibid., III.38

श्रेष्ठोऽर्धं तु हरेत्तत्र भवेत् पादश्च कर्तरि।
पादस्तेषु सभासत्सु यत्र निन्द्यो न निन्द्यते॥

śreṣṭho 'rdhaṁ tu harettatra bhavet pādaśca kartari ।
pādasteṣu sabhāsatsu yatra nindyo na nindyate ॥

— Ibid., III.40

One who is asked about virtue should not reply in a zig-zag manner like a mule wandering about. A king, who gives such a reply (while occupying the seat of a judge) loses both the kingdom and the subjects. He should not be afraid of censuring the wicked. If the wicked are not condemned, the judge gets half the sin, the sinner a quarter of it and audience, the other quarter.

Harsh words must be avoided in a communication. The *Mahābhārata* says:

मर्माण्यस्थीनि हृदयं तथाऽसून्
  रूक्षा वाचो निर्दहन्तीह पुंसाम्।
तस्माद्वाचमुशतीं रूक्षरूपां
  धर्मारामो नित्यशो वर्जयीत॥

marmāṇyasthīni hṛdayaṁ tathā 'sūn
  rūkṣā vāco nirdahantīha puṁsām।
tasmādvācamuśatīṁ rūkṣarūpāṁ
  dharmārāmo nityaśo varjayīta॥

— Ibid., IV.7

Harsh words consume the vital parts of the body, the bones, the heart and the vital breaths. Therefore, a virtuous man should always avoid harsh words.

नाक्रोशी स्यान्नावमानी परस्य
  मित्रद्रोही नोत नीचोपसेवी।
न चाभिमानी न च हीनवृत्तो
  रूक्षां वाचं रुशतीं वर्जयीत॥

nākrośī syānnāvamānī parasya
  mitradrohī nota nīcopasevī।
na cābhimānī na ca hīnavṛtto
  rūkṣāṁ vācaṁ ruśatīṁ varjayīta॥

— Ibid., IV.6

A man uttering harsh words, being acrimonious in disposition, hard hearted, piercing men with wordy thorns, carries the god of death in his tongue.

On many an occasion, silence will be a better way of communication rather than words. The *Mahābhārata* says:

अरुन्तुदं परुषं रूक्षवाचं वाक्कण्टकैर्वितुदन्तं मनुष्यान्।
विद्यादलक्ष्मीकतमं जनानां मुखे निबद्धां निर्ऋतिं वै वहन्तम्॥

aruntudaṁ paruṣaṁ rūkṣavācaṁ
vākkaṇṭakairvitudantaṁ manuśyān ।
vidyādalakṣmīkatamaṁ janānāṁ
mukhe nibaddhāṁ nirṛtiṁ vai vahantam ॥

— Ibid., IV.8

Silence is said to be better than speech. Speech, if at all, should be truthful. Truthful utterance should also be beneficial. Beneficial utterance of truth should conform to the *dharma*. Hence start practising silence first.

An Administrator should seek the wise counsel of the Advisory Committee before taking a decision and communicating it to the general public. The *Mahābhārata* says:

न श्रद्दधाति कल्याणं परेभ्योऽप्यात्मशङ्कितः।
निराकरोति मित्राणि यो वै सोऽधमपूरुषः॥

na śraddadhāti kalyāṇaṁ parebhyo 'pyātmaśaṅkitaḥ ।
nirākaroti mitrāṇi yo vai so 'dhamapūruṣaḥ ॥

— Ibid., IV.19

He is a mean man, who does not listen to the good counsel from others, who is suspicious of himself and repudiates his own friends.

But one should be careful about the counsel. The *Mahābhārata* says:

न निह्नवं मन्त्रगतस्य गच्छेत्संसृष्टमन्त्रस्य कुसङ्गतस्य।
न च ब्रूयान्नाश्वसिमि त्वयीति सकारणं व्यपदेशं तु कुर्यात्॥

na nihnavaṁ mantragatasya gacchetsaṁsṛṣṭamantrasya kusaṅgatasya ।
na ca brūyānnāśvasimi tvayīti sakāraṇaṁ vyapadeśaṁ tu kuryāt ॥

— Ibid., V.27

One should not seek secret counsels of a person who keeps bad company. But he should not drive him away by saying,

"I do not have faith in you." He should withdraw him offering some excuse.

One of the channels of communication available for an administrator is through his/her own subordinates. But he/she should be choosy about people selected for such an important job. The *Mahābhārata* says:

न विश्वासाज्जातु परस्य गेहे
गच्छेन्नरश्चेतायनो विकाले।
न चत्वरे निशि तिष्ठेन्निगूढो
न राजकाम्यां योषितं प्रार्थयीत।।

na viśvāsāñjātu parasya gehe
gacchennaraścetāyano vikāle।
na catvare niśi tiṣṭhennigūḍho
na rājakāmyāṁ yoṣitaṁ prāthayīta।।
— Ibid., V.26

That sort of a servant who when ordered by the master does not pay heed to his words, who when asked to do something replies indifferently, argues to the contrary, is to be dismissed as quickly as possible.

अस्तब्धमक्लीबमदीर्घसूत्रं सानुक्रोशं श्लक्ष्णमहार्यमन्यैः।
अरोगजातीयमुदारवाक्यं दूतं वदन्त्यष्टगुणोपपन्नम्।।
astabdhamaklībamadīrghasūtraṁ sānukrośaṁ ślakṣṇamahāryamanyaiḥ।
arogajātīyamudāravākyaṁ dūtaṁ vadantyaṣṭa-guṇopapannam।।
— Ibid., V.25

The messenger of communication should have presence of mind, boldness, readiness of action, softness of approach, refinement in manners, incorruptibility, sound health and dignified speech.

There should be an element of suggestion in communication. A censure, for instance, conveyed suggestively will be accepted but not the one hurled at a person directly. Lofty ideas will carry weight only when they are conveyed suggestively. The *Bhagavad-Gītā* explains the nature of a *yogin* suggestively thus:

या निशा सर्वभूतानां तस्यां जागर्ति संयमी।
यस्यां जाग्रति भूतानि सा निशा पश्यतो मुनेः॥

yā niśā sarvabhūtānāṁ tasyāṁ jāgarti saṁyamī |
yasyāṁ jāgrati bhūtāni sā niśā paśyato muneḥ | |

— *Bhagavad-Gītā*, II.69

What is night for others is the time the *yogin* keeps awake. The time when others keep awake is the night for a "seeing" *yogin*.

This means that a *yogin* is involved in things beyond this world in which the ordinary men have no interest. The *yogin*, on the other hand, is not interested in the worldly things which attract the attention of the ordinary mortals.

Arthaśāstra also points out certain defects in communication, which have to be avoided. They are *akānti, vyāghāta, punarukta, apaśabda* and *saṁplava* (absence of charm, contradiction, repetition, incorrect use of a word and confusion).

Sl. No.	Avoid	Use
1.	**Absence of Charm**	
	We are pleased to receive your order.	We are in receipt of your order.
2.	**Contradiction**	
	We are honoured to be dishonoured by you.	We regret to be dishonoured by you.

Sl. No.	Avoid	Use
3.	**Repetition** The consensus of opinion is that the tax is unfair.	The consensus is that the tax is unfair.
4.	**Incorrect use of a word** We must take steps to boost the morality of the workers.	We must take steps to boost the morale of the workers.
5.	**Confusion** Knowing that there would be objection to the price we fixed was the reason we fixed a lower price.	The price was lowered in order to avoid objection on its hike.

Illustrations to these can be found in plenty through the words of *vidūṣakas* in Sanskrit drama. The *Doṣa-Prakaraṇa* in the Alaṁkāra works also gives a list of such expressions that are to be avoided. For example:

कुतः कान्तारवृत्तीनां कार्तार्थ्यार्थित्वमस्ति नः।
kutaḥ kāntāravṛttīnāṁ kārtārthyārthitvamasti naḥ।
— *Pratāparudrīya*, V. line between 19 and 20

When will he attain the fulfilment of his desires? Here the word *kārtārthyarthitva* is harsh to hear, which results in "absence of charm."

अरण्यमहिषोदग्रविषाणोदर जन्मनाम्।
महत्यर्घेऽपि मुक्तानां स्त्रियो मुक्ताविभूषणाः॥

araṇyamahiṣodagraviṣāṇodara janmanām।
mahatyarghe 'pi muktānāṁ striyo muktāvibhūṣaṇāḥ॥
— Ibid., V.84

In the forest, the womenfolk decorated themselves with pearls that were procured from the horns of the bisons.

Here the possibility of getting pearls from the horns of the bisons is contradictory to nature.

जीर्णकाननसंकीर्णे विन्ध्ये काननवृत्तयः।
jīrṇakānanasaṁkīrṇe vindhye kānanavṛttayaḥ।
— Ibid., V.29

In the worn out forests of Vindhyā, forest life was taking place. (Here the repetition of the word *kānana* (forest) does not carry any significance.)

कदा भविष्यते वासः।
kadā bhaviṣyate vāsaḥ। — Ibid., V.14

Here the word *bhaviṣyate* is grammatically wrong:

विहाय च गृहांस्तान् वै व्यत्यस्त वन वृत्तयः।
कदा भविष्यते वासः कटकेषु महीभृताम्॥

vihāya ca gṛhāṁstān vai vyatyasta vana vṛttayaḥ।
kadā bhaviṣyate vāsaḥ kaṭakeṣu mahībhṛtām॥
— Ibid., V.14

Will the kings get back to their city (kaṭaka) life? (Here confusion arise due to another meaning of the work *kaṭaka*, that is, mountain.)

Arthaśāstra also gives a list of 32 devices for preparing a document (like *adhikaraṇa*, *vidhāna* and *yoga*). The topic of the document is to be decided first. Then the contents have to be listed. In an official document, technical terms may be used; therefore, the terms used in the document must be defined. The reason for the issue of the document is to be stated and explained. References are to be given wherever necessary. Possible doubts may be raised and answered in the course of the explanation. Illustrations are to be given for important points. The *prima facie* view and the established view must be clearly brought out.

अधिकरणम्, विधानम्, योगः, पदार्थः, हेत्वर्थः, उद्देशः, निर्देशः, उपदेशः, अपदेशः, अतिदेशः, प्रदेशः, उपमानम्, अर्थापत्तिः, संशयः, प्रसङ्गः, विपर्ययः, वाक्यशेषः, अनुमतम्, व्याख्यानम्, निर्वचनम्, निदर्शनम्, अपवर्गः, स्वसंज्ञा, पूर्वपक्षः, उत्तरपक्षः, एकान्तः, अनागतावेक्षणम्, अतिक्रान्तावेक्षणम्, नियोगः, विकल्पः, समुच्चयः, ऊह्यम् इति।

adhikaraṇam, vidhānam, yogaḥ, padārthaḥ, hetvarthaḥ, uddeśaḥ, nirdeśaḥ, upadeśaḥ, apadeśaḥ, atideśaḥ, pradeśaḥ, upamānam, arothāpattiḥ, saṁśyaḥ, prasaṅgaḥ, viparyayaḥ, vākyaśeṣaḥ, anumatam, vyākhyānam, nirvacanam, nidarśanam, apavargaḥ, sasaṁjñā, pūrvapakṣaḥ, uttarapakṣaḥ, ekāntaḥ, anāgatāvekṣaṇam, atikrāntāvekṣaṇam, niyogaḥ, vikalpaḥ, samuccayaḥ, ūhyam iti।

— *Arthaśāstra*, XV.3

The 32 devices are : 1. Selection of a topic; 2. Statements of contents; 3. Employment of technical terms; 4. Reasons for issuing the document; 5. Mention of rules; 6. Explanation; 7. Caution; 8. Reference; 9. Application; 10. Indication; 11. Analogy; 12. Doubts; 13. Similar situations; 14. Precedence; 15. Corollary; 16. Agreement; 17. Derivation of terms; 18. Illustration; 19. Exception; 20. *Prima facie* view; 21. Established view; 22. Future Proposal; 23. Restrictions; 24. Options, 25. Date of issue; 26. Time limit; 27. Conditions; 28. Remedy; 29. Issuing authority; 30. Medium; 31. Summary; and 32. Conclusion.

The order in which the items are stated may need some revision. But they are all relevant and are applicable to the modern times as well.

It is clear, therefore, that the principles of communication were known to the ancient Indians and were put to effective use in the official circles as well as in literary works as seen from the examples cited in this chapter.

4

Human Resource Management

Human Resource

A COMPANY is generally made up of three "M's" and an "H." They are machine, material, money and human resource. Men/women can handle the other three but none of these can handle men/women. Even men/women find it difficult to handle other men/women, since every human being is individualistic and is guided by his/her emotions. When men/women are trained, guided and controlled properly, they can do wonders. Human resource is, therefore, the most vibrant component of an industry. If men/women are motivated, they can rise to great levels and exhibit their individuality and creativity. Different men/women have different talents and attitudes. A manager has to assess the merit of each person and select suitable persons for the respective jobs. A good plan given in the hands of wrong persons will end in failure and loss. It is, therefore, necessary to select the right persons and delegate power to them.

Staffing

It is always difficult to select competent people for jobs. Some may have the qualification but not the experience or vice versa. A company should attract qualified and experienced people and train them to suit its needs. Having got the training and experience, the persons concerned may opt to join other companies. It takes a lot of time, energy and money to train people. If they leave, the company stands to lose. Therefore, they have to be maintained. Staffing consists of all these factors, namely, securing, recruiting, selecting, training, appraising and maintaining the staff.

According to McFarland, staffing is the function by which managers build an organization through the recruitment, selection and development of individuals as capable employees.[1] Some scholars add a few more functions like compensating, retirement and maintaining favourable conditions of work.

For the appointment of staff, the manager of thc respective departments should be given full freedom so that they can build a team for themselves. Men/women appointed as regular staff and trained will exhibit better loyalty than those who are simply hired for a job. Realizing the importance of staffing, many companies that earlier had a department called personnel department, now call it human resource department. While the personnel department deals with such routine matters as transfers, retirements, relieving, selection and recruitment, the human resource department lays more emphasis on training, development, orientation, motivation and employer-employee relationship.

Staffing should not be considered as an ad-hoc measure to fill in vacancies; it is a continuous process to develop a team in each department. Members are ready to unite as a team if their needs (as referred to in Maslow's theory) are better understood. The manager, as a team leader, is expected to take care of these aspects in the staffing function. The team members have to be assured that they are important for the company. If a manager possesses an autocratic attitude and says, "Do as I say. You are paid for doing what I say. Do not

---

1. McFarland Dalton, p. 238.

ask questions," the subordinates will lose their morale. Their interest will only be on wages/salary and consequently their work culture will suffer. In staffing, the accent should not only be on the present but also on the future. The idea should be on building future team leaders and therefore, even while recruiting, efforts should be taken to select resourceful and enterprising people who will have the future of the company in mind.

Identification of manpower requirements is another aspect of staffing. In many cases, two or more people will be doing the same work resulting in idle manpower. There could also be certain cases where a single person who is considered efficient is loaded with enormous work. Consequently, fatigue sets in and his/her efficiency suffers. Delegation of work and division of labour are very important aspects of management. They should be taken into account while identifying manpower requirements.

There are two ways of recruiting people for middle-level jobs. One way is to identify talents within the company and promote them. By this process, the lower-level staff get motivated to perform. Having been in the company for a few years, they identify themselves with the company and work towards the goal. It is easier to build a team with the existing people. There is also a disadvantage in promoting insiders. As the proverb goes "familiarity breeds contempt," insiders tend to take things easy, which leads to lethargy and complacency. On the other hand, if people are appointed from outside the company, they will have a new-found zeal to perform. The desire to establish themselves in the company will motivate them to perform better. The disadvantage is that they will take time to adjust themselves to the new environment and learn the procedures followed in the new company. Moreover, the existing people are likely to develop a suspicion and may hesitate to co-operate with the newly appointed people. There could, therefore, be a judicious mixture of both the policies in a company; there should be a balance between promotion of insiders and recruitment from outside. While specialists could be invited from outside for some of the sophisticated jobs, existing people could be promoted for routine jobs. Manpower planning is thus an important area as observed by Edwin B. Geisler who says,

> Manpower planning is a process (including forecasting, developing, implementing and controlling) by which a firm ensures that it has the right number of people and the right kind of people at the right place and the right time for things for which they are economically most useful.[2]

It will be interesting to note that Sanskrit literature also reflects the same opinion in several places.

Human Resource Planning

Manpower planning or human resource planning (HRP) has assumed a greater importance in the present-day situation on account of fast changing needs of a company. There are frequent changes in the wake of stiff competition from similar companies, technological developments, the demands of the markets and the products and the unpredictable nature of consumer behaviour.

If a machine becomes obsolete, it can be discarded in a dustbin or dumped in the godown. But a human being cannot be treated like this. People have to be trained to adjust themselves to any new development. Even if some employees have to be retrenched, under extraordinary circumstances, the company concerned has to pay them compensation. In

2. Edwin B. Geisler, "Manpower Planning — An Emerging Staff Function", *Management Bulletin*.

order to avoid such unpleasant situations, a careful study of the manpower requirements must be made. Companies have to devise a plan to appoint qualified persons, who will be able to adjust themselves to future changes and demands of the company. There should be adequate staff to take care of the regular working of the company. Every member should rise to the occasion or step into the shoes of somebody who is not available and get things done in a satisfactory manner. This will be possible only if the satisfaction level of the employees is high. According to Dale S. Beach,

> Manpower planning is a process of determining and assuring that the organization will have an adequate number of qualified persons, available at the appropriate times, performing jobs which meet the needs of the entire enterprise and which provide satisfaction for the individuals involved.[3]

All the points mentioned by the author refer to manpower planning or HRP on a long-term basis to realize the goals and objectives of a company. The major aims of HRP[4] are to ensure that the company —

(i) Obtains and retains the quality and quantity of manpower it needs,

(ii) Makes the best use of its manpower resources, and

(iii) Is able to anticipate the problems arising from potential surpluses or deficits of manpower.

HRP consists of four basic steps:

(i) Determining the organizational objectives,

(ii) Assessing the skills and expertise required to realize the organizational objectives,

3. Dale S. Beach, Chapter 3.

4. Michael Armstrong, Chapter 5.

(iii) Taking stock of the existing manpower and planning for additional requirements, and

(iv) Planning for future needs of human resources.

Every company has its own goals and objectives. An awareness should be created among all the employees on the objectives of the company. Newly recruited people should also be educated about the goals of the company. They should all be oriented to the goal and guided in the proper direction. This is an important aspect of HRP.

It is expected of every manager to determine the skills and expertise required to meet the objectives of the company. Keeping in view the possibility of future changes in the company, suitable persons with varying skills and capabilities must be selected. It is not enough if the employees possess the skill that is expected of them. Their skills must be properly channellized by the managers for the benefit of the company.

Every department in a company engages itself in forecasting the results in order to plan for its development and progress. The sales department analyses the results of the previous year and forecasts what could be its level for the current year. Accordingly, targets are fixed and efforts are taken to reach the target. In the staffing function also, such forecasting and planning are necessary. Just as a stores department keeps a constant watch on its inventory, the HR department also is required to keep an inventory of skills and make frequent assessment of the employees performance, strength, weakness, capability, the ability to improve and their efficiency level. Employees who show promise may be encouraged with promotion. Taking into consideration all these factors, it should be possible for managers to predict human resource requirements and plan accordingly for a specific period. In the process of manpower planning, a manager will have to do the exercise of "job analysis." In other words, he has to make an assessment of total number of jobs within the company, available skills and additional skills required to handle the jobs. Job analysis consists of job description and job specification. Job description takes into consideration job content, working environment, and terms and conditions of employment. Job specification is the identification of skill, knowledge and abilities required to perform a particular job efficiently and effectively.

Career development of employees is yet another important step in HRD. Monotony and frustration set in if the employees are asked to perform the same jobs over and over again. If there are avenues for their career development, they will show improvement in their jobs. As part of the career development plan, employees can be offered challenging jobs, career counselling and participation in workshops.

In spite of careful HRP, certain drawbacks may still occur on account of identity crisis of the employees, lukewarm attitude of the top-level management, lack of co-ordination among the departments, communication gap and fast changing technology. A manager is expected to anticipate all these problems and take steps to solve them.

Training

Life is a continuous learning process. An employee spends a major part of his/her life in a company. It is the duty of every management to provide ample scope for the employees to learn something new every year. Training improves the efficiency of the employees and gives them self-confidence and job satisfaction. Training need not be totally conventional; it could be innovative depending upon the needs of an organization. It can alter the mindset of employees and bring about an attitudinal change in them. It can mould the behaviour of the workers and orient them towards organizational goals. For the management, it is an investment for the future. It creates a proper environment for a healthy work culture within the organization. Training is also helpful in proper handling of equipments, thus reducing risks.

Training is a learning process and therefore it follows all the principles of learning. Thus training is an active process involving all the faculties of a human being. In training, the trainee must have guidance (through a trainer). In those cases wherein an employee is left to fend for himself/herself, he/she learns by a trial-and-error method. But this is a costly as well as a dangerous process. If experts in the field guide the employees, they can learn quickly and correctly. Before embarking on training, the management should motivate the employees toward training and create an interest in them. Otherwise, the efforts of training would prove futile. Incentives should be provided for trainees to take up their training seriously. Standards should be set and the trainees should be evaluated on their performance.

Training is classified into on-the-job training and off-the-job training. For example, apprenticeship is an on-the-job training. Off-the-job training is conducted outside the work spot. It could be conducted by a special institute meant for the purpose. There could be lectures, group discussions, seminars, role-playing and case studies in an off-the-job training.

Performance Appraisal

All organizations are action-oriented and an assessment of the actions performed is always necessary while planning for further growth. Without a proper feedback, it is not possible to know exactly where we stand and what step should be taken next. Likewise, performance appraisal is necessary for all managements to know about the potential of the workers and the work that is turned out by them. In short, it is an evaluation process. It is a way of realizing one's own strengths and weaknesses. It is also a statement showing the opportunities given, seized, lost and found. It can also speak about challenges, threats and problems faced and how they were tackled. It assists the managers to make quality assessment of the work done by the employee and take decisions on promotions and incentives. It helps in identifying potential performers, who can be groomed to take up additional responsibilities. It can thus be a tool for HRP. While judging the performance of employees through performance appraisal, the subjective element is removed. In other words, there will be no room for favouritism. Performance appraisal will also be helpful in identifying the non-performers and work-shirkers. If they have to be sent out and if compensation has to be paid, the performance appraisal will be helpful in deciding the quantum of compensation.

Though the performance appraisal seems to be a good administrative measure in many respects, it has certain disadvantages as well. If the manager dealing with the appraisal resorts to favouritism or undue criticism, the appraisal will not reflect the true picture. It will create suspicion in the minds of the employees. It may affect the employee-manager relations and may lead to tension in the organization. Suspicion and tension will lead to inefficiency and loss of morale. Some organizations, therefore, opt for self-appraisal where an employee makes an assessment of his/her own self. Here again, the employee may try to boost his/her own rating, by giving false statement but supervisors and managers can do the cross-verification and make an assessment. In spite of a few drawbacks, which are bound to be there in any system, performance appraisal can be an effective tool in the evaluation of employees. The appraisal forms should be structured carefully so as to avoid any subjective element. It can be improved upon every year based on the experience of previous years, so that it is made simple, straightforward and objective.

Sanskrit Sources on Human Resource Management

The *Arthaśāstra* discusses the HRP, *HRD* and training in the first two books. Topics such as appointment of ministers, councillors, chaplain, testing the integrity of employees, appointment of secret servants, rules for the envoys and guarding against rebellion are discussed in these chapters.

In the eighth chapter of the first book, there is an interesting discussion on whether former classmates could be appointed. Bhāradvāja supports their appointment since their integrity and capability are well known. They also enjoy the confidence of the chief. Another scholar by name Viśālākṣa opposes this view and says that having been playmates, they do not care much for the authority of the chief. Only like-minded persons must be appointed. The followers of Parāśara say that new persons are likely to divulge secrets and therefore, persons who have helped during calamities should be appointed since their loyalty is proven. But this is only devotion and not a trait of intellect, says a teacher by name Piśuna. According to him, those who are capable of bringing income to the treasury through their well-thought-out tasks must be appointed. But Kauṇapadanta refutes this view and says that enhancing the income is only one aspect of a minister. Therefore, hereditary people, sons and grandsons of those who had served the chief's father (or grandfather) must be appointed since their conduct is well known. They will never desert him even when scolded by the chief. "No" says Vātavyādhi, "for, bringing everything under their control, they begin to act as masters themselves and therefore new persons who have studied the text well alone should be appointed. They will function without fear or favour." One by name Bahudantiputra opposes this view on the ground that mere theoretical knowledge is not enough to run the administration. Those with practical knowledge and those who are endowed with nobility of birth, intellect, integrity, bravery and loyalty must be appointed.

Kauṭilya concludes the discussion by saying that the best of all these arguments must be taken. The capacity for doing a work is important and other considerations should not intervene in the appointment of suitable people. All these people may be appointed but they should be assigned appropriate duty depending upon their calibre. They should be given ranks accordingly and posted for a particular duty, place and time.

Kauṭilya uses two terms, namely, *amātya* and *mantrin*, both of which are loosely translated as "minister." But in Kauṭilya's terms, the former refers to the minister while the latter has the sense of "counsellor." A minister may simply carry out the orders of the king but a counsellor advises the king on several important issues.

A counsellor must be a native of the country, so that he will have first-hand knowledge of the problems of the people. He will know the language, tradition and culture of the land. He must be of noble birth so that he will be accepted by the people. He should be easy to hold in check, trained in the arts, possessed of sharp intellect, persevering, dexterous, eloquent, bold, possessed of a ready wit, endowed with energy and power, able to bear troubles, upright, friendly, devoted, endowed with good character, strength, health and spirit, devoid of rigidity and fickleness, amiable and not given to creating animosities. One who possesses 100 per cent of these qualities will be an able counsellor. If he has only 75 per cent of it, he will be useful for middle-level jobs. One having 50 per cent of the qualities may be given low-level jobs.

Kauṭilya also gives an idea on how to test a counsellor:[5]

Quality	To be tested
1. Nationality, nobility of birth	Through his kinsmen
2. Training in arts, etc.	By experts in the field
3. Intelligence, perseverance and dexterity	By his handling of undertakings
4. Eloquence, presence of mind and boldness	By engaging him in conversation
5. Energy, power, ability to bear troubles	By his management during a calamity
6. Uprightness, friendliness and devotion	From his dealing with others
7. Character and strength	From those living with him
8. Amiability, absence of animosity	By personal observation

The affairs of an administrator are *pratyakṣa* (directly perceived), *parokṣa* (unperceived) and *anumeya* (inferred). What is directly seen by an administrator is *pratyakṣa*. What is communicated by others is *parokṣa*. Forming an idea of what has not been done through what is done is *anumeya*. An administrator must resort to all these three for judging the performance of the counsellors, since their activities are manifold and take place simultaneously at several places.

5. *Arthaśāstra*, I.9.3.

The integrity of the ministers must be tested frequently through secret agents. A minister should pick-up a feigned quarrel with the king and then approach a new minister who is to be tested. The counsellor should abuse the king and instigate the minister to join a rebel group. If the minister repulses the idea, he is loyal.

The commander-in-chief may approach the minister and offer material gains. If he repulses the suggestion, he is upright.

The queen's female attendant may approach a minister and say that the queen is in love with him. If he repulses the idea, he is pure. This is a test of lust.

By prior arrangement, some of the existing ministers should organize a feigned conspiracy meeting. The new minister should also be invited. At the height of the discussion, the police forces should enter and arrest all of them. The ministers should devise a plan to escape and kill the king. If the new man resists or repulses the idea, he tests against fear and can be declared loyal.

Those who pass the test of piety may be appointed in the judiciary. Ministers passing the test of material gains may be posted as the director of stores, those passing the test of lust may be appointed for a job inside the palace and those passing the test of fear may be posted for duties near the king. Those who pass all the tests may be promoted as counsellors. Those who fail in one or two tests may be employed in far off places like mines and forests.

Kauṭilya also gives a series of tests for the appointment of secret agents. Some of these may not be relevant for the present-day situation. But it may be noted that politicians and administrators seek the services of secret agents even today.

Kauṭilya emphasizes the importance of counselling since all undertakings should be preceded by consultation. The place where the discussions are held must be kept secret. It should be held at a secluded place. What is discussed must not be heard even by birds. No unauthorized person should be allowed near the place of discussion. In fact, it will be ideal to have discussions through sign language and gestures.

How should an administrator deliberate on a confidential matter? If he discusses it with others (even with very close counsellors), it will not remain a confidential matter anymore. The information may leak out somehow. We have had instances of cabinet decisions and even the budget being leaked out, in recent history. Therefore, an administrator should deliberate alone over a confidential matter, says Bhāradvāja. But Viśālākṣa refutes this argument and says that there is no merit in the deliberation by a single person. The affairs of an administrator are threefold: directly perceived, unperceived and inferred. Coming to know of what is known, confirming what has become known and removal of doubt in case of two possible alternatives in a matter — all these can be achieved only through discussions with ministers and counsellors.

An administrator should despise none and should listen to the opinion of every individual. He should make use of the sensible words of even a child.

But Parāśara is not satisfied with the argument as it does not say how the secrecy of the discussion can be maintained. The administrator, therefore, may convene a meeting of the counsellors, pose some hypothetical questions similar to the problem on hand and seek their opinion. Even if it leaks out, it does not matter since it is only a hypothetical problem.

"No" says Piśuna, for, the counsellors, being questioned about a hypothetical problem will give their opinion in a different manner. Therefore, the administrator should deliberate with those who are approved for the particular undertaking. Each will know only part of the problem. Thus opinions are collected, maintaining secrecy at the same time.

"This is not a good proposal" says Kauṭilya. Consultation should be held with three or four counsellors who are aware of the entire problem. Only then, a lasting solution can be given by them.

Holding consultation with a single person is rather dangerous. He will assume airs and will behave as he pleases without restraint. There is a danger in holding consultation with just two. They may conspire together and bring about the downfall of the administrator himself. With three or four, such chances are minimized. With more counsellors, it becomes a crowd and so no fruitful decision can be reached. However, in conformity with time, place and work to be done, the administrator should deliberate with one or two, depending upon their competence. In times of calamity, he should call all the ministers and counsellors for discussion.

Kauṭilya speaks of five aspects of a deliberation. They are: (i) means of starting the undertaking, (ii) the excellence of men and material, (iii) suitable appointment in relation to place and time, (iv) provision against failure, and (v) accomplishment of the work.

Kauṭilya then speaks of the rules for the envoy, which may serve as a guideline for the ambassadors and officers of the foreign services. They can also be helpful to the company secretaries who act as the spokesmen of the companies. An envoy should observe graciousness in speech, exchange pleasantries and possess knowledge of all activities in the area of operation. He should have a quick grasp of the subject. While visiting an opponent's area, he should make a quick assessment of his strengths and weaknesses. He should not make a show of his own strength and be prepared to put up with even disagreeable words. He should avoid women and drink. He should sleep alone, for the intentions of a person are revealed in sleep or intoxication.

Kauṭilya also speaks of rules for the king, which may be applicable to the present-day administrators.

When the administrator is active, the employee becomes active following the master's example. He should divide his time into eight parts. One part should be allotted for estimating the income and expenditure. During the second, he should look into the affairs of all those who are under his care. The third part must be allotted for his study and updating of knowledge. The fourth part must be allotted for assigning tasks to the heads of the departments. During the fifth, he should communicate with various sections of the official circle. The sixth part must be allotted for discussions with various heads. The seventh part must be allocated for private thinking and chalking out plans. The eighth must be set apart to know about what is taking place in the competitors' place (for a king, the enemy's place).

All urgent matters have to be settled immediately. An affair postponed becomes difficult to settle or even impossible to settle.

Kauṭilya refers to three sources of income, namely, current, outstanding and derived from other sources. What comes from day-to-day business is current. What belongs to the preceding year or what is transferred from another sphere of activity is the outstanding income. What is lost and written off, fine imposed on employees, extra income, compensation for loss, gifts and property that is confiscated from others are the income from other sources. Balance due to disbandment (undertakings wound up) and undertakings given up (sick units) is return from expenditure.

An administrator has to organize the maintenance of record books. The record books must contain details of the amount of increase or decrease in the use of materials, expenses, excess, surcharge, wages for casual workers, price of commodities, articles of high value, low value and forest produce, laws, transactions, customs, expenditure towards special allowances, remedial measures taken during sudden calamities, etc. The books should contain revenue, income and expenditure, balance statements for audit and customs.

The qualities expected of the director of trade (*paṇyādhyakṣa*), as given by Kauṭilya are worth noting here. The director of trade should be conversant with the differences in the prices of commodities of both high and low value and the popularity of both high and low value or the demand for goods of various kinds, whether produced on land or in water and whether they have arrived along the land routes or water routes and also suitable times for resorting to dispersal or concentration, purchase or sale.

If a particular commodity is available in plenty, a large quantity of it must be stored somewhere so that the price level can be maintained.

He should see to it that there is no short supply of goods. He should prevent traders from getting unreasonable profit that may be injurious to the common people. He should not create a restriction on sale of goods and at the same time prevent a glut in the market with respect to goods that are always in demand. The director of trade should fix appropriate price for goods so that neither the people nor the traders are put to difficulties. He should arrange import of goods if necessary. Exemption from taxes should be given for goods that are brought by ships. No law-suit in money matters should be allowed against foreign traders.

While assessing the profit of the sale of foreign goods, all expenses for duty, road tax, escort charges, ferry dues, food and fodder should be taken into account.

The collector of customs and tolls (*śulkādhyakṣaḥ*) should establish the customs house in the vicinity of the main gates of the city. A flag facing east or north should be hoisted on the roof. The officers should record details about traders, the place from which they are coming, the type of merchandise they have brought and its quantity. They should also check the identity pass (where it has been issued and by whom) and the stamping made on them. Those who do not carry valid documents should pay double the dues. Likewise, those who under-quote the quantity or the price shall be fined heavily. Those who hike the price unreasonably shall also pay double the duty in addition to the fine imposed on them. Duty exemption is granted for goods meant for marriage, marriage gifts for the bride, goods meant for religious sacrifice or ceremony or temple worship or rituals. A trader making a false declaration on these is liable for punishment.

Some goods like weapons, armours, metals, chariots, jewels, grains and cattle are prohibited from being exported. The director of customs should cut out goods that are harmful to the country and those that are worthless. He should offer duty-free facility to highly beneficial imported goods and seeds that are rare.

Kauṭilya also deals with the duties of the superintendent of textiles, the director of agriculture, the controller of spirituous liquor, supervisor of slaughter house, the controller of shipping, the superintendents of cattle, horses, elephants, chariots, foot-soldiers, passports, pastures and the city superintendent quite elaborately. Many of them may be useful for the present-day managers of the respective activities.

Motivation

Motivation is an important area of HRM, since a company has to deal with human beings belonging to different environments and different backgrounds. Men/Women are known for their complex behavioural patterns and attitudes. It is the duty of a HR manager to tackle these problems, many of which can be solved through counselling, motivation and proper encouragement. A company has different levels of employees like workers, skilled assistants, supervisors and so on. Each section and sometimes each individual has to be approached in a different style and motivated. It is, therefore, necessary for a manager to know the various issues involved in motivation like:

(i) acceptance of legitimate authority,
(ii) organizational commitment,
(iii) motivation through counselling,
(iv) motivation by challenge,
(v) relationship with subordinates,
(vi) rewards,
(vii) leadership qualities, and
(viii) self-motivation.

The *Kaṭhopaniṣad*[6] speaks of two aspects of life: *śreyas* and *preyas*, the former being what is beneficial to us and the latter, what is liked by us. All that is liked by us may not be beneficial to us.

A sugar patient, for example, may be craving for sweets, but they may turn out to be killers in his case. Children hate to take medicine but it is beneficial to them. A similar idea is

---

6. अन्यच्छ्रेयोऽन्यदुतैव प्रेयस्ते
उभे नानार्थे पुरुषं सिनीतः।
तयोः श्रेय आददानस्य साधु भवति
हीयतेऽर्थाद्य उ प्रेयो वृणीते।।

→

set forth in the *Rāmāyaṇa*:

स हि कल्याणचरित्रः कैकेय्याः आनन्दवर्धनः।
करिष्यति यथावद् वः प्रियाणि च हितानि च॥
ज्ञानवृद्धो वयो बालो मृदुर्वीर्यगुणान्वितः।
अनुरूपः स वो भर्ता भविष्यति भयापहः॥

sa hi kalyāṇacaritraḥ kaikeyyāḥ ānandavardhanaḥ ।
kariṣyati yathāvad vaḥ priyāṇi ca hitāni ca ॥
jñānavṛddho vayo bālo mṛdurvīryarguṇānvitaḥ ।
anurūpaḥ sa vo bhartā bhaviṣyati bhuyāpahaḥ ॥
— Ayodhyā Kāṇḍa, 45, v 7 & 8

Rāma decides to go to the forest in spite of everybody else trying to prevent him. He wants to motivate people with his own example to adhere to truth and *dharma*. The poet here enunciates the qualities expected of a motivator, like *kalyāṇa carita* (spotless character); *priyāṇi kariṣyati hitānica* (doing what is beneficial to others); *vayasā bālaḥ, jñānato vṛddhaḥ* (young in age but mature in knowledge); *mṛdu vīraḥ* (although gentle, yet bold); *bhayāpahaḥ* (removing all fears and anxieties).

As for organizational commitment, there cannot be a better illustration than what is stated in *Abhijñānaśākuntalam*:

भानुः सकृद्युक्ततुरङ्ग एव
रात्रिंदिवं गन्धवहः प्रयाति।
शेषः सदैवाहितभूमिभारः
षष्ठांशवृत्तेरपि धर्म एषः॥

→ *anyacchreyo 'nyadutaiva preyaste*
ubhe nānārthe puruṣaṁ sinītaḥ ।
tayoḥ śreya ādadānasya sādhu bhavati
hīyate 'rthādya u preyo vṛṇīte ॥
— *Kaṭhopaniṣad*, I.2.1

bhānuḥ sakṛdyuktaturaṅga eva
rātriṁdivaṁ gandhavahaḥ prayāti ।
śeṣaḥ sadaivāhitabhūmibhāraḥ
ṣaṣṭhāṁśavṛtterapi dharma eṣaḥ ।।
— V.4

The Sun has yoked his horses but once (after which he goes on and on), the wind keeps wafting day and night. Ādiśeṣa bears the earth ever and anon (so is the role of an administrator).

For a king, the kingdom is *svahasta dhṛta daṇḍamiva ātapatraṁ*,[7] that is, it is like an umbrella of which a man carries the staff in his own hand, does not so much remove fatigue as it causes tiresomeness. Similarly, for an administrator, his work will not be a bed of roses. He has to make sacrifices for the sake of the work that he is doing.

To practise that kind of a selfless attitude, one has to draw a lesson from nature, as Kālidāsa would put it.

भवन्ति नम्रास्तरवः फलागमैः
नवाम्बुभिर्भूरिविलम्बिनो घनाः।
अनुद्धताः सत्पुरुषाः समृद्धिभिः
स्वभाव एवैष परोपकारिणाम्।।

bhavanti namrāstaravaḥ phalāgamaiḥ
navāmbubhirbhūrivilambino ghanāḥ ।

---

7. औत्सुक्यमात्रमवसादयति प्रतिष्ठा
क्लिश्नाति लब्धपरिपालनवृत्तिरेव।
नातिश्रमापनयनाय यथा श्रमाय
राज्यं स्वहस्तधृतदण्डमिवातपत्रम्।।
autsukyamātramavasādayati pratiṣṭhā
kliśnāti labdhaparipālanavṛttireva ।
nātiśramāpanayanāya yathā śramāya
rājyaṁ svahastadhṛtadaṇḍamivātapatram ।।
— *Abhijñānaśākuntalam*, V.6

anuddhatāḥ satpuruṣāḥ samṛddhibhiḥ
svabhāva evaiṣa paropakāriṇām॥

— Ibid., V.12

Trees bend low when they are laden with fruits, clouds hang low down while bearing fresh rain drops; good men are never elated over riches; this is the very nature of the munificent people.

We have an excellent specimen of good counselling in Śukanāsā's advice in Bāṇa's *Kādambarī*.[8]

The kings are deceived by rogues intent on achieving their selfish ends; they are the vultures in seizing the fish of

---

8. अपरे तु स्वार्थनिष्पादनपेरेर्धनपिशितग्रासगृध्रैरास्थाननलिनीबकैर्द्यूतं विनोद इति, परदाराभिगमनं वैदग्ध्यमिति पानं विलास इति गुरुवचनावधीरणमपरप्रणेयत्वमिति, परिभवसहत्वं क्षमेति, स्वच्छन्दता प्रभुत्वमिति, देवावमाननं महासत्त्वतेति, तरलतोत्साह इति दोषानपि गुणपक्षमध्यारोपयद्भिरन्तः स्वयमपि विहसद्भिः प्रतारणकुशलैर्धूर्तैर-मानुषोचिताभिः स्तुतिभिः प्रतार्यमाणा सर्वजनस्योपहास्यतामुपयान्ति दर्शनप्रदानमप्यनुग्रहं गणयन्ति। दृष्टिपातमप्युपकारपक्षे स्थापयन्ति। आज्ञामपि वरप्रदानं मन्यन्ते।

तदेवंप्रायेतिकुटिलकष्टचेष्टासहस्रदारुणे राज्यतन्त्रेऽस्मिन्महामोहकारिणि च यौवने तथा प्रयतेथा यथा नोपहास्यसे जनैर्न निन्द्यसे साधुभिर्न धिक्क्रियसे गुरुभिर्नोपालम्भसे सुहृद्भिर्न शोच्यसे विद्वद्भिः। यथा च न प्रकाश्यसे विटैर्न प्रतार्यसे कुशलैर्न वञ्च्यसे धूर्तैर्न प्रलोभ्यसे वनिताभिर्नापिह्रियसे सुखेन।

apare tu svārthaniṣpādanapererdhana piśitagrāsagṛdhrairā-sthānanalinībakairdyūtaṁ vinod iti, paradārābhigamanaṁ vaidagdhyamiti pānaṁ vilāsa iti guruvacanāvadhīraṇam-aparapraṇeyatvamiti, paribhavasahatvaṁ kṣameti, svacchandatā prabhutvamiti, devāvamānanaṁ mahāsattvateti, taralatotsāha iti doṣānapi guṇapakṣamadhyāropayadbhirantaḥ svayamapi vihasadbhiḥ pratāraṇakuśalairdhūrtairamānuṣocitābhiḥ stutibhiḥ pratāryamāṇā sarvajanasyopahāsyatāmupayānti darśanapradānamapyanugrahaṁ gaṇayanti। *dṛṣṭipātamapyupakārapakṣe sthāpayanti*। *ājñāmapi varapradānaṁ manyante*।

tadevaṁprāyetikuṭilakaṣṭaceṣṭāsahasradāruṇe rājyatantre 'smin-mahāmohakāriṇi ca yauvane tathā prayatethā yathā nopahāsyase janairna nindyase sādhubhirna dhikkriyase gurubhirnopālambhase suhṛdbhirna

→

> wealth. Calling gambling a diversion, drinking a delightful sport, rejection of elders advice as independence, putting up with insults as patience, wantonness as the exercise of authority, insulting the great as superior might, and restlessness as enterprise, they raise the vices to the rank of virtues and laugh within themselves. Thus deluded by the rogues, the kings whose minds are intoxicated with pride of wealth, behave as though they are superhuman beings. They consider even granting of an interview as a favour, a glance as a benefit conferred and even the issue of an order as the granting of a boon.
>
> You should behave in such a way that you are not censured by the good, not condemned by elders, not reproached by friends, not pitied by the learned and not laughed at by the knaves, not duped by the crafty, not shattered by the rogues, not deluded by women and not carried away by pleasures.

Most of the points addressed to the kings are applicable to the present-day managers, particularly, to the HR managers.

Motivation through counselling or advice may sometimes prove counter-productive. A better way would be to throw a challenge to people and motivate them to take it up manfully and accomplish it.

While in exile in the forest, Draupadī chides the Pāṇḍavas for their lethargy and goads them to action against the enemies.

पुरः सरा धामवतां यशोधनाः
सुदुःसहं प्राप्य निकारमीदृशम्।

→ *śocyase vidvadbhiḥ* । *yathā ca na prakāśyase viṭairna pratāryase kuśalairna vañcyase dhūrtairna pralobhyase vanitābhirnāpahriyase sukhena* ।

Kādambarī — Śukanāsā advice, ed. M.R. Kale, Motilal Banarsidass, 1968, p., 174ff.

भवादृशाश्चेदधिकुर्वते रतिं
निराश्रया हन्त हता मनस्विता॥

puraḥ sarā dhāmavatāṁ yaśodhanāḥ
suduḥsahaṁ prāpya nikāramīdṛśam।
bhavādṛśāścedadhikurvate ratiṁ
nirāśrayā hanta hatā manasvitā॥
— *Kirātārjunīya*, I.43

If men like you who regard glory as their wealth and who are the foremost among the high-spirited, resort to contentment after having met with such an insult, very difficult to bear, then alas! sealed is the fate of the high-minded, being rendered supportless.

Bhīma also supports the view of Draupadī and says:

विपदोऽभिभवन्त्यविक्रमं रहयत्यापदुपेतमायतिः।
नियता लघुता निरायतेरगरीयान्न पदं नृपश्रियः॥

vipado 'bhibhavantyavikramaṁ rahayatyāpadupetamāyatiḥ।
niyatā laghutā nirāyateragarīyānna padaṁ nṛpaśriyaḥ॥
— Ibid., II.14

Calamities overwhelm a man devoid of powers; future forsakes one smitten by calamities; degradation is the certain lot of one who has no bright future; prosperity which depends on valour does not abide with inactivity.

One of the motivating factors in an organization is the unbiased functioning of the chief.

When Bhīma persuades Yudhiṣṭhira to take immediate action against the enemies, the latter first appreciates his views by saying,

अपवर्जितविप्लवे शुचौ हृदयग्राहिणि मग्लास्पदे।
विमला तव विस्तरे गिरां मतिरादर्श इवाभिदृश्यते॥

apavarjitaviplave śucau hṛdayagrāhiṇi maṅgalāspade।
vimalā tava vistare girāṁ matirādarśa ivābhidṛśyate॥
— Ibid., II.26

Your pure and honest intention is clearly seen reflected in your speech which is free from arguments contrary to reasoning and proof, lucid, attractive to the heart and salutary, as a mirror which is free from the coating of dust, transparent, charming to the mind and auspicious.

सहसा विदधीत न क्रियामविवेकः परमापदां पदम्।
वृणुते हि विमृष्यकारिणं गुणलुब्धाः स्वयमेव संपदः॥

sahasā vidadhīta na kriyāmavivekaḥ paramāpadāṁ padam।
vṛṇute hi vimṛṣyakāriṇaṁ guṇalubdhāḥ svayameva saṁpadaḥ॥
— Ibid., II.30

Arguments have been advanced keeping in view the aggressive tactics of the enemies. There is no room for contradiction in the political wisdom revealed. Who can make such a quick assessment through a speech that is highly motivating?

The social and organizational environments are the vital motivating factors, so also the satiation of the needs. The rewards are also helpful in boosting the morale of an individual.

We have a very good example from *Kirātārjunīyam*. In order to win over the subjects to his side, Duryodhana adopts several tactics.

अनुपालयतामुदेष्यतीं प्रभुशक्तिं द्विषतामनीहया।
अपयान्त्यचिरान्महीभुजां जननिर्वादभयादिव श्रियः॥

anupālayatāmudeṣyatīṁ prabhuśaktiṁ dviṣatāmanīhayā ।
apayāntyacirānmahībhujāṁ jananirvādabhayādiva śriyaḥ ॥
— Ibid., II.10

Having suppressed his arrogance, he treats his subordinates as if they were his affectionate friends. His friends are treated as close relatives and relatives as if the entire kingdom had been handed over to them.

प्रभवः खलु कोशदण्डयोः कृतपञ्चाङ्गविनिर्णयो नयः।
स विधेयपदेषु दक्षतां नियतिं लोक इवानुरुध्यते॥

prabhavaḥ khalu kośadaṇḍayoḥ kṛtapañcāṅgavinirṇayo nayaḥ ।
sa vidheyapadeṣu dakṣatāṁ niyatiṁ loka ivānurudhyate ॥
— Ibid., II.12

He adopts the fourfold policies of *sāma* (conciliation), *dāna* (giving gifts), *bheda* (sowing differences), and *daṇḍa* (punishment) very judiciously. The policy of conciliation is always followed by the offer of gifts. Gifts are made with due honours and conferring of honour is distinguished by due regard to virtues and merits.

The best aspect of motivation is self-motivation. Financial rewards do not last long. People increase their wants and continue to suffer. Craze for money and desires can never be satisfied. Some financial rewards will only kindle the desire for more and more such rewards. Likewise, position and power have their own limitations. So the best way to motivate people is to make them enjoy their work. If they are trained to work for the sake of work without expecting rewards, self-motivation can be inculcated. Hence, the *Bhagavad-Gītā* says:

You have the right to do the work only and not to aspire for the results. At the same time do not have attachment towards non-work (inertia, laziness).

This is the essence of *karma-yoga*. The Lord further says:

योगस्थः कुरु कर्माणि सङ्गं त्यक्त्वा धनञ्जय।
सिद्ध्यसिद्ध्योः समो भूत्वा समत्वं योग उच्यते।।

yogasthaḥ kuru karmāṇi saṅgaṁ tyaktvā dhanañjaya।
sidhyasidhyoḥ samo bhūtvā samatvaṁ yoga ucyate।।

— II.48

Perform your duties, remaining in the state of *yoga*, relinquishing attachment and remaining indifferent to success and failure; such equanimity is called *yoga*.

The Lord further says that one should treat pleasure or pain alike; victory or defeat alike; profit or loss alike.

सुखदुःखे समे कृत्वा लाभालाभौ जयाजयौ।
ततो युद्धाय युज्यस्व नैवं पापमवाप्स्यसि।।

sukhaduḥkhe same kr̥tvā lābhālābhau jayājayau।
tato yuddhāya yujyasva naivaṁ pāpamavāpsyasi।।

— Ibid., II.38

In short, one should be a *sthitaprajña*, one of noble mind, a state which is achieved by the control of sense organs. In this state, the mind remains unperturbed, thirst for pleasures disappears and passion, fear and anger are driven away.

An orientation toward such a state of mind will surely bring about wholesome change in the attitude of the employees of an organization.

A better interpersonal relationship would prevail, leading to better understanding among all sections of employees of the organization.

Lord Kṛṣṇa gives the essence of work culture in one cryptic statement *yogaḥ karmasu kauśalam.*[9] Whatever may be the nature of work one is doing, one should attain perfection in it. Swami Vivekananda says, "Even if you are a cobbler, you must be the best cobbler in the world." One should concentrate on three aspects of work, namely *lāghavam* (smartness), *sāmarthya* (ability) and *kṛtaniścayatva* (determination), to achieve perfection in work. We may find it difficult to drive a nail on a plank but a carpenter does it quite smartly. A violinist elegantly plays a tune on the violin, but for a novice, the same violin strikes only discordant notes like a scorpion bite. If you hit a cricket ball with all your might, it may fall at your own feet while a trained cricketer drives it gracefully to the boundary with effortless ease. This is smartness. Very often we see that if a batsman is determined to stay at the crease, runs come automatically. The ability to do a work efficiently comes by training and practice. Practice makes a man perfect, it is said. Constant practice turns into ability. Hence all these three, namely, *lāghava, sāmarthya* and *kṛtaniścayatva* are essential for the successful completion of a task. All these three are very important from the point of view of HRM.

It is a matter of common experience that when a person joins an organization, he/she has abundant enthusiasm to prove himself/herself and impress all the superiors. But in course of time, his/her enthusiasm wanes and his/her performance level dips considerably. Such people pick-up vices or divert their attention towards other fields of interest. The reason for this is that they fall a prey to some of the de-motivating factors like lack of promotion or incentive, peer pressure, fault-finding

9. बुद्धियुक्तो जहातीह उभे सुकृतदुष्कृते।
तस्माद्योगाय युज्यस्व योगः कर्मसु कौशलम्॥
buddhiyukto jahātīha ubhe sukṛtaduṣkṛte |
tasmādyogāya yujyasva yogaḥ karmasu kauśalam ||
— Ibid., II.50

by the superiors, monotony of work, wrong understanding of the principles of the union, mismatch between qualification and experience, arrogance, inferiority complex, fear of authority and lack of motivation to take up responsibilities. Some people who are given to jealousy, anger, malice and ill-will also turn out to be under-achievers.

Most of these de-motivating factors can be traced to two areas: (i) emanating from the self, and (ii) occurring within the organization. The first one is nothing but ego. Most of the personality clashes can be traced to the ego problem. It arises due to the dictates of the mind. It is said, *mana eva manuṣyāṇāṁ kāraṇaṁ bandha mokṣayoḥ;* it is the mind which is responsible for the states of being free or being bound. Texts like the *Bhagavad-Gītā*, therefore, advocate the control of the mind. If the mind is allowed to reflect too much on the words of another, for example, the angry words of the manager, vengeance and a desire to retaliate develops. Therefore, the mind has to be controlled. A fitting reply could be given politely without arousing anger in others. Advaita philosophy advocates the principles of non-difference between the individual souls at the absolute level. If the mind is trained toward such a state, the words of another will not affect any individual. There is no state as an individual ego. In fact, there is no ego at all. Such a high-sounding philosophy may be beyond the level of understanding of workers or even managers. But, if put into practice slowly, some of the problems related to personal ego could be solved. But, indeed, the Advaita philosophy is rather difficult to follow for common people. Ancient Indian philosophers have also suggested an alternative solution to such ego problems. It may appeal to the common people as well. They recommend two related concepts namely, *bhakti* and *śraddhā*. *Bhakti* may be translated as devotion or dedication but it has a wider sense than these two terms. Ego clashes arise only when we attach ourselves to work and its result. If the work and the result are dedicated to the Supreme Being without an iota of attachment and if the personal element is removed, then the ego does not raise its head. If the work is considered as God's work, there is a desire to do it as perfectly as possible. By attributing the results also to God, undue expectation of personal benefits and consequent corruption are totally warded off. *Śraddhā*, literally means faith, faith in oneself. Swami Vivekananda asked, "What is the use of believing 33,000 gods if you do not have faith in yourself?" Self-belief and unshakable faith in oneself lead to self-confidence. Faith and confidence help a person to progress towards perfection. A number of mythological stories bring out the efficacy of *bhakti* and *śraddhā*.

We have the instances of Prahlāda, Dhruva, and Mārkaṇḍeya, who had immense *bhakti* towards God and thereby attained the highest liberated state. The story of Viśvāmitra's relentless efforts to attain the Brahmarṣi status, which he ultimately achieved, brings out the effect of *śraddhā*.

The *Pañcatantra* consists of fables that are didactic in nature. They are full of wisdom and lofty ideas that are helpful to the present-day HR manager dealing with human resources, machines and money. The title of one of the *Pañcatantra* fables is *mitralābha*, meaning bondage of friendship. The employer-employee relationship also should be viewed as a bond between the two. The employer should take care of the welfare of the employee, who in turn should give out his/her best for the company and contribute to its growth. He/She should feel that when the company grows, he/she also grows. A pithy stanza from *Pañcatantra* brings out this idea.

न विना पार्थिवो भृत्यैर्न भृत्याः पार्थिवं विना।
तेषां च व्यवहारोऽयं परस्परनिबन्धनः।।

na vinā pārthivo bhṛtyair na bhṛtyāḥ pārthivaṁ vinā ।
teṣāṁ ca vyavahāro 'yaṁ paraspara nibandhanaḥ ॥
— *Pañcatantra*, I.87

There must be bonds of union in all their dealings, since no prince (employer) lacks his servants, nor servants lack a prince.

अरैः सन्धार्यते नाभिर्नाभौ चाराः प्रतिष्ठिताः।
स्वामी सेवकयोरेवं वृत्तिचक्रं प्रवर्त्तते॥

araiḥ sandhāryate nābhir nābhau cārāḥ pratiṣṭhitāḥ ।
svāmi sevakayorevaṁ vṛtticakraṁ pravartate ॥
— Ibid., I.89

Many spokes support the hub which keeps them all in grip. Only this way, rolls the wheel of master-servant relationship.

The master-servant relationship will be a healthy one, only if both the parties realize that (i) without one, the other one cannot function, (ii) their relationship is a mutually beneficial bond, and (iii) unless each supports the other, they cannot forge ahead.

All these principles are amply illustrated in the *Pañcatantra* stories.

Another *Pañcatantra* stanza implies that

फलार्थी नृपतिर्लोकान्पालयेद्यत्नभास्थितः।
दानमानादितोयेन मालाकारोङ्कुरानिव॥

phalārthī nṛpatirlokānpālayedyatnabhāsthitaḥ ।
dānamānāditoyena mālākāroṅkurāniva ॥
— *Pañcatantra*, I. 223

An employer expecting good results must care for and nurture the employees with money and honour, as a gardener would the seeds, with water and manure.

It is not the monetary consideration alone that can satisfy a worker. His/Her pride and honour are more important to him/her than money. If they are satisfied, he/she will give out his best. The verse says:

राजा तुष्टोऽपि भृत्यानर्थमात्रं प्रयच्छति।
ते तु संमानमात्रेण प्राणैरप्युपकुर्वते।।

rājā tuṣṭo'pi bhṛtyānarthamātraṁ prayacchati।
te tu saṁmānamātreṇa prāṇairapyupakurvate।।

— *Pañcatantra,* I. 83

A master who is pleased gives away only money. But a servant when honoured helps his master even by giving his life (for the master).

Recognition of merit is another aspect of HRM. The *Pañcatantra* says:

न तच्छस्त्रैर्न नागेन्द्रैर्न हयैर्न पदातिभिः।
कार्यं संसिद्धिमभ्येति यथा बुद्ध्या प्रसाधितम्।।

na tacchastrairna nāgendrairna hayairna padātibhiḥ।
kāryaṁ saṁsiddhimabhyeti yathā buddhyā prasādhitam।।

— *Pañcatantra,* I. 125

A business is not so well established by means of weapons etc. as when brought about by the merit of talent.

Meritorious persons must be encouraged through better placements and promotions. The *Pañcatantra* says:

स्थानेष्वेव नियोक्तव्याः भृत्याश्वाभरणानिच
न हि चूडामणिः पादे प्रभवामीति बध्यते।।

sthāneṣveva niyoktavyāḥ bhṛtyāśva ābharaṇāni ca।
na hi cūḍāmaṇiḥ pāde prabhavāmīti badhyate।।

— *Pañcatantra,* I.136

> Servants, horses and gems have to be placed at their appropriate places only. A crest jewel is not tied to the foot just because you can afford.

If a gem that is fit to be set in a golden setting, is set in tin, the gem is not going to complain. It will only speak of the foolishness of the wearer.

The *Pañcatantra*, therefore, emphasizes that right persons should be employed at the right places.

It may not always be possible to get the right people for the right places. By proper training, motivation and encouragement even ordinary people who would have been mediocre in the beginning may turn out to be useful employees. A person who is found as a misfit at a particular position may shine in another department. It is for the employer to unearth the talent of each and every person, accommodate him at the appropriate place and derive the best out of him. The *Pañcatantra* says:

अश्वः शस्त्रं शास्त्रं वीणा वाणी नरश्च नारी च।
पुरुषविशेषं प्राप्ता भवन्ति अयोग्यश्च योग्यश्च॥

aśvaḥ śastraṁ śāstraṁ vīṇā vāṇī naraśca nārī ca।
puruṣaviśeṣaṁ prāptā bhavanti ayogyaśca yogyaśca॥

— Ibid., I.124

> In the case of a horse, book, sword, woman, man, lute and word, their usefulness or uselessness depends on the qualities the user lends to them.

Though money may not serve as a lasting motivating factor, negation of monetary benefits will be detrimental to the interests of the organization. What is due for the employees must be settled as and when they are due. Denial or even delaying of benefits will demoralize the employees. A demoralized employee can never give out his best. The productivity-linked incentive schemes usually prove effective to boost the morale of the employees. The *Pañcatantra* says,

कालातिक्रमणं वृत्तेर्यो न कुर्वीत भूपतिः।
कदाचित्तं मुञ्चन्ति भर्त्सिता अपि सेवकाः॥

kālātikramaṇaṁ vṛtteryo na kurvīta bhūpatiḥ।
kadācittaṁ muñcanti bhartsitā api sevakāḥ॥
— *Pañcatantra*, I. 155

If a master does not delay payment to the servants, they will never leave him even when scolded or threatened.

Every human being in this world wants happiness, peace and tranquillity. But when it comes to action that leads to peace and happiness, men/women get into all kinds of confusion and doubt. Knowing fully well that a particular action is harmful, still a person indulges in it. A Sanskrit verse puts it very beautifully:

पुण्यस्य फलमिच्छन्ति पुण्यं नेच्छन्ति मानवाः।
न पापफलमिच्छन्ति पापं कुर्वन्ति यत्नतः॥

puṇyasya phalamicchanti puṇyaṁ necchanti mānavāḥ।
na pāpaphalamicchanti pāpaṁ kurvanti yatnataḥ॥

Men desire the fruit of meritorious actions but do not acquire merits. They do not desire the fruits of sin yet with diligence perform sins only.

Everybody wants money and position but people do not direct their efforts towards acquiring them. The world does not provide free lunch for anybody; one has to struggle hard to achieve something. The workers in an establishment must be told about these points so that they do not cherish the idea of quick money. Hence, scriptures emphasize the importance of *satya* (truth), *dharma* (virtue) *vinaya* (humility), *tyāga* (sacrifice) and *tapas* (austerity).

A number of Western scholars have conducted experiments and have come up with fresh and new theories on human psychology. The ancient Indian scholars have also made equally creditable progress in understanding human psychology. Their methods have been quite successful in shaping the minds of millions of people over centuries. Almost till the middle of the last century the entire mass of Indian people were guided by the principles of *dharma, puṇya,* and *pāpa*. Corruption and deceit were practically non-existent, so much so that most of the houses never had bolts for the doors, which were always kept open. In the name of economic development, materialism and consumerism have become deep rooted in the society, leading to avariciousness and self-centredness. It is necessary, therefore, to train modern managers not only on Western theories but also in Indian traditions. A new indigenous orientation could be given to students in HRM as suited to Indian conditions so that our managers can serve the society in a better fashion.

5

Centres of Power

Power and Authority

MANAGEMENT specialists draw a distinction between Power and Authority. While power is the ability to do something, authority is the right to do it. Power needs no formal position while authority needs one. Power may be derived from many sources while authority is derived from organizational position only. Power is a broad concept. It may step in when authority fails to produce the desired results. Power is a concept in itself while authority is only a source of power. Authority is essential in an organization since human beings have a tendency to subject themselves to authority for social and security needs. Men/Women are controlled by such factors as variable nature, unstable mind and unpredictable behaviour. Authority is helpful in combining the efforts of human resources towards achieving the organizational goals.

Why is Authority Needed?

A group of individuals alone cannot run an organization. Direction, guidance, control and decision making are necessary to channellize the efforts of several individuals. Power has to be vested with one individual to take decisions. Taking even wrong decisions is better than no decision and inaction. A group of individuals can discuss a matter but ultimately one person has to take a decision. Hence, all establishments have power centres and hierarchy in authority. In a manufacturing firm, the production department will be more powerful. In a supermarket, the sales section is more powerful. The centre of power varies from one organization to the other. In the same organization, power may shift from one department to another depending upon the situation. In some organizations, the unions may be very powerful and they may dictate terms to the management who may succumb to pressure every time the union comes up with a proposal. Even so, the authority to issue an order lies only with the top-level management. In some organizations, most of the decisions may have to be taken as per the direction of the legal department which will be more powerful than other sections since "knowledge is power." In a chemical laboratory, the laboratory assistant may be more powerful than a newly appointed scientist, since he (the laboratory assistant) may have acquired considerable knowledge out of years of experience.

Manager's Role as an Authority

A manager is vested with power in a particular area of operation. A manager is not the one who does things by himself/herself; he/she has to get things done through others. He/She must therefore delegate powers to others equitably to get the work done. But he/she must retain the authority to take decisions. A manager can exercise authority only when he/she has knowledge, power of influencing others, competence, leadership skill and responsibility. A manager must be more knowledgeable than his/her subordinates in order to gain their respect and recognition of his/her authority. Otherwise, they will upstage him/her and expose his/her inefficiency. A manager must be an influential leader. Some are influential by their skill, some by their eloquence, some by their physical appearance and some through their money power. A manager can influence others by his/her skill, knowledge and ability to guide others in times of crisis.

Likewise his/her competence and leadership skills will always stand him/her in good stead in exercising his/her authority. Authority may not always bring credit. When there is a setback or a reverse, only the manager will be held responsible though personally he/she would not have done anything wrong. Authority and responsibility are two sides of the same coin.

Types of Authority

(i) **Traditional:** In the family, for example, traditionally, authority rests with the father.

(ii) **Reputation:** The reputation a person holds in the society may be responsible for his/her authority. For example, a frail-looking religious leader or a temple priest may be very powerful in a village on account of the magical or mystical powers attributed to him/her by others.

(iii) **External:** An organization may be controlled by the legislation and court orders in a number of issues. It cannot go against them. These are the external authorities.

(iv) **Functional authority:** An authority can come from the function that is carried out by a person. For example, in the village the local school principal may have some authority on account of his/her function as the caretaker of the children of the village.

Acceptance of Authority

Authority has no relevance unless it is accepted by all those concerned. Why should people accept an authority? The reasons may be varied but ultimately it boils down to one thing, that is, the person who is wielding authority possesses something which others do not have. A small illustration may make it clear. A group of dozen boys of about the same age had a small cricket team. One of them held authority over others. If he said "out" (even if it was not so) others would accept it without questioning. He would bat or bowl as long as he liked and others would get a chance only when he was tired. If anybody questioned his authority, he would immediately call off the game and pack up since the ball, bat and stumps belonged to him.

Workers subject themselves to the authority of the MD since it is he/she who owns the plant and the machinery and it is he/she who has invested money in the company.

Another reason for accepting authority is the natural tendency of majority of the people to shy away from responsibility. Authority means responsibility, and why should a person bother himself/herself by taking additional responsibility? At one stage, in the banks, a number of clerks declined promotion as officers and continued as clerks for certain obvious reasons. First, as a clerk, he/she can wind up his/her work with the accounts books by 3 p.m. An Officer has to stay till all the books are tallied and the work may go up to 7 p.m. Second, if the offer is accepted, he/she would be transferred to a remote place. Moreover, the margin of benefits is not much. Generally speaking, economic considerations, family upbringing, fear complex and inferiority complex are responsible for the acceptance of authority.

Limits of Authority

No power or authority is unlimited in this world. Only the God Almighty has unlimited powers and is therefore omniscient, omnipresent and omnipotent. As for the human beings, the factors that limit the power of authority in a company are:

(i) Government rules and regulations,
(ii) Legal provisions, contracts, agreement,

(iii) Collective bargaining power of workers through unions,
(iv) Social beliefs, customs and habits,
(v) Internal policies, procedures, rules,
(vi) Financial constraints, and
(vii) Rigidity of approach.

Power Dynamics

"Power dynamics" refers to the distribution of power among the persons concerned or constituent departments. Some points of power dynamics are worth noting:

(i) There can be little or no rationale behind power distribution, for example, the PA to a minister may be more powerful than the minister himself. In some small companies, the managing director's wife may be more powerful than the MD himself.

(ii) People in power are tempted to grab more and more power.

(iii) Power corrupts and absolute power corrupts absolutely.

(iv) Power keeps shifting. For example, several years back, when Bajaj was the only good scooter available in the country, people were prepared to register and wait for 3 or 4 years. So in the Bajaj company the sales manager had no power at all. The production manager was more powerful than others. In periods of uncertainty also, power shifts. During the strike period, the union leader becomes very powerful.

(v) Dependence is also responsible for accumulation of power.

Sanskrit Sources on Power and Authority

According to *Arthaśāstra*, power is threefold: (i) *mantra-śakti* — the power of counsel, (ii) *prabhu-śakti* — power of might, and (iii) *utsāha-śakti* — power of energy.[1]

MANTRA-ŚAKTI

The power of counsel arises from knowledge. In many kingdoms those days, the chief minister was more powerful than the king himself. Thus we find Yaugandharāyaṇa, the trusted minister of King Udayaṇa proudly declaring:

> प्रारम्भेऽस्मिन्स्वामिनो वृद्धिहेतौ
> दैवेनेत्थं दत्तहस्तावलम्बे।
> सिद्धेर्भ्रान्तिर्नास्ति सत्यं तथापि
> स्वेच्छाकारी भीत एवास्मि भर्तुः।।
>
> *prārambhe 'sminsvāmino vr̥ddhihetau*
> *daivenettham̐ dattahastāvalambe*।
> *siddherbhrāntirnāsti satyam̐ tathāpi*
> *svecchākārī bhīta evāsmi bhartuḥ*।।
> — *Ratnāvalī*, I.8

When this enterprise conducive to my master's progress (devised by me) is thus given support by destiny, truly there is no apprehension about success; yet acting, as I do, of my own free will, I am a little afraid of my master.

The minister had heard a prophecy that the prince, who marries Ratnāvalī, the daughter of the king of Ceylon will become the sole emperor of the entire world. So he wants to bring about the marriage of his master with this princess, though the king is already married to Queen Vāsavadattā. His efforts to bring the princess of Ceylon to the mainland meet with a disaster since the ship in which she has been sent is wrecked. But the princess somehow reaches the shore, holding on to a broken wooden plank. By his clever manoeuvres, the minister brings

1. See *Arthaśāstra*, chapters 6 and 9 on *Prabhu-śakti* and *Mantra-śakti*.

about the union of the two.

Though the ministers were powerful in some of the kingdoms, generally, the king had the final say in all matters. He would, of course, discuss all matters with the ministers before taking a final decision.

PRABHU-ŚAKTI

Prabhu-śakti or the might of power results in two ways: (i) by the superior power of the self, and (ii) by the depletion of power of the opposite camp. In a tennis match, for example, both the players may be erratic, but one of them wins on account of the higher number of unforced errors committed by the opponent. In business circles, the competitor is the opponent. Every company is expected to make an analysis of Strength, Weakness, Opportunity and Threat (SWOT Analysis) not only of its own position but also that of the competitor. A manager has to make an assessment of the relative strength and weakness of power, place, time, labour problems, profit, loss, balance sheet and share market of his/her company and that of the competitor.

UTSĀHA-ŚAKTI

The power of valour is called *utsāha-śakti*[2] Bravery, rising against insult, quick action and dexterity are its qualities.

Kauṭilya indulges in a discussion on the relative strength of the power of might and the power of energy. Scholars in the field say that energy is superior. For, an administrator himself/herself, if brave, strong, healthy and well-trained, is able to conquer the power of might on account of his/her spirit. But an administrator without energy, though possessed of might, perishes when overpowered by valour.

---

2. *Arthaśāstra*, 6.2.33 ff.

"No," says Kauṭilya. The king possessed of might surpasses the king possessed of energy by his might or by taking the help of another king superior to him in energy, or by hiring or purchasing heroic men.

The situation in which a king is placed cannot be totally compared with that of an executive in a company, but there are still many points from Kauṭilya's discussions that are useful to the present-day managers.

"Of the powers of might and counsel, might is superior, for barren wisdom without might is useless and such a king is ruined just as the lack of rains ruins the seeds sown in the soil," say the other scholars.

"No," says Kauṭilya, "the power of counsel is superior. For, the king with eyes of intelligence and knowledge is able to take counsel and overreach enemies possessed of might and energy by conciliation and other practices."

Some of these points may be useful in the tangles between the management and the union or in the case of one company with another.

Success attends on an administrator who is able to handle power, place and time effectively. Some scholars feel that power is superior to the other two since a man endowed with power can overcome the difficulties of even hostile terrain and extreme conditions of heat and cold. (For example, a cricketer endowed with a good technique will be able to negotiate difficult pitches under difficult conditions (extreme heat or cold) anywhere in the world.) "Place is superior," say some, "for, a dog on land can drag a crocodile and a crocodile in water drags a dog. "Time is superior," say some others, "by day, a crow kills an owl and at night an owl kills a crow." "No," says Kauṭilya. Power, place and time are mutually helpful.

How can one acquire power. There is no consensus on this issue and it is very difficult to pinpoint the means. Anyhow three of them that are important may be stated.

(i) By turning out extraordinary work.

(ii) By doing the right thing at the right time. One must be effective as well as efficient. Effectiveness is doing the right things. Efficiency is doing things right.

(iii) By coalescing with others. For example, some years back, the Velvet shampoo introduced shampoo in small sachets, sold it for one rupee each and made it popular among the poor people too. But they did not have market network. So they gave the marketing rights to Godrej company who have a well established network. It was a great success.

Arthaśāstra stresses on the importance of good alliance for an administrator who is desirous of retaining power. It prescribes six qualities for a good ally.

नित्यं वश्यं लघूत्थानं पितृपैतामहं महत्।
अद्वैध्यं चेति संपन्नं मित्रं षड्गुणमुच्यते।।
nityaṁ vaśyaṁ laghūtthānaṁ pitṛpaitāmahaṁ mahat ।
advaidhyaṁ ceti saṁpannaṁ mitraṁṣaḍguṇamucyate ।।
— Ibid., 7.9 37 ff

An ally should exhibit the qualities of constancy, trust-worthiness, obedience, resourcefulness and faithfulness, by virtue of holding a hereditary position and further he should also be a person of certain greatness and not indulging in double dealing.

These qualities are applicable to partnership in a company. Partnership should be made with people who have a firm mind. Fickle-minded people join as partners today and break the partnership tomorrow for some flimsy reason. They are not fit for partnership. In a partnership, if both are working partners, it will work well. If one is a working partner and the other a sleeping partner, the former will hold more power. It is ideal to have a partner under our control. A partner should be able to quickly mobilize resources. Otherwise the partnership will suffer. In a family business, the members of the family will be partners. If our powers are depleted, it will be beneficial to seek the partnership of a powerful person and control the sinking ship. Trust and integrity are the hallmarks of a partnership. A person with double dealings is not fit for partnership.

How to remain in power? Kauṭilya deals with this topic quite elaborately.

Ability to Cope with Uncertainty

Impoverishment, greediness and dissatisfaction should not rise among the subjects (in our context, employees). A suitable hike in emoluments (e.g., DA rise) should be given to the employees to meet the rise in cost of living. Impoverishment leads to greediness. We see that when there is short supply of some goods, the shopkeepers tend to hoard the available stock and sell it for a higher price. If their genuine grievances are not attended to, employees lose faith in an administrator and they become disaffected towards him/her. Kauṭilya therefore insists that impoverishment, greediness and disaffection should not rise, and if they rise, immediate remedial measures are to be taken to alleviate the sufferings of the subjects.

Control of Strategic Contingencies

When faced with challenges, a company should take contingency measures to meet the challenge. For example, when the manufacturers of Surf faced stiff challenge from the competitors, they diversified the product by manufacturing Super Surf and Surf Excel.

Kauṭilya speaks of six measures of foreign policy. They are *sandhi* (pact), *vigraha* (war), *āsana* (staying quiet), *yāna* (marching), *dvidhābhāva* (dual policy) and *saṁśraya* (surrender).[3] In a pact, one's freedom is curtailed to a certain extent. War involves expenditure and loss of human beings and material. A contingency plan would be *āsana,* when one goes neither for a war nor for a pact. He keeps his eyes open and watches the movements of the opposite camp, improving his own resources at the same time. When the chips are completely down, one may surrender unto a superior force and make the best out of a bad bargain. Sometimes one has to take things lying low. One may stoop only to conquer later. Even under the worst circumstances, contingency plans have to be drawn to tide over the crisis.

Sensitivity to People's Perception

An administration should be sensitive or responsive to the hopes and aspirations of its employees. Only then, it can retain its power. If the employees become disillusioned, they may leave the company. Without employees what is a company worth its name?

Kauṭilya recommends that a king should cater to the needs of the people and see that they do not become disenchanted with their ruler. If life becomes difficult for them, they will migrate to the neighbouring countries. Without people, what can the country yield, like a barren cow going dry?

Efforts to Stabilize the Power on Hand

It is always difficult to retain power rather than acquire power

3. *Arthaśāstra*, 7.1.

because people around will always try to grab the power of one who has it. Hence, an administrator should be intent on keeping his/her power in tact and should never give room for complacency.

To see That People are Behind us Always

The power of a person is decided by the number of people who are behind him/her in the pecking order. Every department in a company will try to see that other departments are behind them always and not overtake them. The production manager, for examplc, will not produce more than what is necessary and pile up the stock. He will produce only that much as is necessary so that the marketing manager will always be behind him asking for finished products to be marketed. To sustain power, an administrator should see that people are behind him/her (in a state of dependence) and not too close to him/her either. Kālidāsa says thus, about Dilīpa.

भीमकान्तैर्नृपगुणैः स बभूवोपजीविनाम्।
अधृष्यश्चाभिगम्यश्च यादोरत्नैरिवार्णवः॥

bhīmakāntairnṛpaguṇaiḥ sa babhūvopajīvinām।
adhṛṣyaścābhigamyaśca yādoratnairivārṇavaḥ॥
— *Raghuvaṁśa*, I.16

By his royal qualities that created a respectful fear in their minds, he was accessible to people but at the same time his presence was awe inspiring like the ocean possessing pearls and sea animals (and also awe inspiring).

Power is associated with leadership qualities since there cannot be a leader without power. This leads us to the discussion on leadership which is taken up in chapter 6.

6

Leadership

Definition of Leadership

LEADERSHIP is defined as the process of influencing group activities toward the accomplishment of goals in a given situation. A leader is a person, who is capable of leading his/her group members in all the activities with regard to goal formation and goal accomplishment.[1]

The definition presupposes that for any person to emerge as a leader, a group is necessary. Leaders do not evolve from vacuum. It is the group which evolves a leader who has influenced the group to do so. It is the group that gives the authority to the leader. The leader motivates the group and unites them for a formidable task. Successful leaders do not instruct. They act and set an example for others to follow. A leader must be capable of taking good decisions, resolving differences among minor groups and integrating them into a cogent group.

Manager as a Leader

The manager of every department is a leader since the employees under him/her expect his/her orders and carry them out as per his/her instructions. An insider, for example, a supervisor, may be promoted as a manager in which case he/she would have already known the members of the team.

---

1. Hersey, Paul and K.H. Blanchard, p. 156.

If he/she is an outsider, a manager has to study the composition of his/her group, the individual qualities of each member of the team and must create a friendly atmosphere for his/her group members to function effectively. He/She must be able to counsel his/her team members if they have a problem, remove the barriers of communication and channellize their efforts. Man is controlled by emotions and therefore a manager has to provide a buffer for the emotional imbalances of the people of his/her group. A manager, as a leader, is vested with the powers to get the work done. A successful leader (manager) is one who uses his/her powers judiciously for achieving the organizational goals. It is said that a person who works hard finds time for everything. The manager, as a leader, has to manage his/her time very efficiently and apportion his/her time equitably for all his endeavours. The managers will definitely be subject to stress and strain but they have to overcome it by anticipating problems in advance and finding solutions for them.

A leader is one who never fights shy of facing problems. In fact, it is usually a crisis situation that brings the best out of a leader. It is not enough if a manager manages the situations; he/she has to lead the team members to a better position. A manager can become a good leader if he/she is able to influence people to constructive work without pressurizing them. He/She uses his/her authority without making people realize that he/she is doing so. A manager should not be a person who is seen once a while issuing orders from an ivory tower. He/She should be seen guiding people all through the day-to-day activities, solving problems then and there. In a company, the union leaders may be from outside and they will not be accountable for majority of the decisions taken, but a manager as a leader is accountable for all the activities taking place in his/her department.

Leadership Styles

Based on the behaviour of the supervising authority, leadership styles are classified into autocratic, democratic and free-rein. The advantage of an autocratic leadership is that it paves the way for quick decisions, but it may produce a demoralizing effect on the followers, who may not be aware of the goal to be reached. Consequently, performance level is likely to dip. The democratic style may be called consultative leadership. In this case, the team members are taken into confidence in decision making and therefore, their involvement is likely to be high. It can lead to job satisfaction among the employees and their morale will also be high. One possible disadvantage in this style is that it is difficult to pin the responsibility if something goes wrong. In the free-rein style, complete delegation of authority is given effect and the total responsibility is in the hands of the employees. The leader just monitors their progress and gives guidance now and then. This style of functioning looks good on paper. But in practical circumstances, such a style may not be feasible since, in our country, the workers are not sufficiently educated and they still lack the maturity to handle crisis situations.

Theories on Leadership

The discussions on what makes a person different from others have been going on among anthropologists, philosophers and psychologists for the past 200 years and some important theories have come up in the course of such discussions.

TRAIT THEORY

Leaders differ from others on account of some traits like intelligence, maturity of ideas and actions, inner urge to forge ahead of others and a concern for others. One of the criticisms against this theory is that some of the people who possess such qualities do not become leaders. There is no uniformity of opinion on the number of traits and which can be considered "leadership traits."

BEHAVIOURAL THEORY

While the trait theory aims at explaining what the leaders are, behavioural theory tries to evaluate leaders on what they do. In other words, this theory is based on the behaviour of leaders. For example, majority of the leaders are able to establish a rapport with the rank and file, communicate with them and get the feedback from them. They are ablc to form a team and rally the members around to doing a constructive work.

SITUATIONAL THEORY

According to this theory, neither the trait nor the behaviour brings out the true qualities of a leader. It is a particular situation that evolves a leader. Under normal circumstances, a leader may behave like an ordinary person. But in a critical situation, he/she rises to the occasion and accomplishes what others fail to do or hesitate to do. While others panic during a crisis, the prospective leader remains cool, analyses the situation and acts boldly. He/She is flexible, listens to the views of others and acts democratically. He/She is friendly, enthusiastic, co-operative and helpful. He/She keeps others interested in him/her but sees at the same time that the followers do not come too close to him/her. Thus he/she prevents others from knowing his/her weaknesses.

What are the situations that throw up a leader. The characteristic of the group is one of them. If the group is confused, the leader may take advantage of this and project himself/herself. He/She can transform them into a cohesive group and make them act. Work environment is another factor. For example, if the working conditions are in an appalling state, the union leader takes advantage of it, turns the minds of the workers against the management and convinces them that he/she would be their saviour. The workers follow him/her like a flock of sheep.

When a group remains in a confused state, not knowing what to do, the leader steps in and guides them towards a goal. In certain cases, the group members may be willing to do a job but they may be unable to do it due to various reasons. A leader demonstrates to the group and trains them to do a job. By this, he/she gets accepted as a leader. In certain other cases, the members may be capable of doing a job but are unwilling to act. At this stage, a leader motivates them, removes their doubts and makes them act. He/She participates in the task and provides a model for others. Some members may be capable and are also willing to do the job. But they hesitate to take up the task and keep waiting for orders from the superior authority. In such cases, it is the duty of the leader to delegate responsibilities to them and make them act.

Some leaders may have the exclusive task of decision making. Before taking a decision, a leader makes an assessment of the effect of his/her decision in the group. In an organization, some decisions may be routine and some may have a far-reaching consequence. But every decision has to be taken after careful consideration. For example, changing the duration of lunch break from one hour to half an hour may be a small decision. The workers may go home half an hour earlier. But it may create a flutter among the workers. They may feel that their freedom of movement is curtailed.

The next point is the acceptance of a decision by the group concerned. It is not enough if a leader takes a decision. He has to talk to the group, convince them of the need for this particular decision and explain the advantages they are likely to get. For example, when the computers were introduced in LIC, there was large-scale protest from the employees. They thought that they would lose their jobs. But when the management explained to them that it was meant to make their job easier, they gradually accepted it. Now the employees feel that the computer is an essential tool.

The third factor that makes a group accept a decision is the amount of time required to make the decision. In the same case of introduction of computer in LIC, the manager assured the workers that the computers would be introduced only in a phased manner and that the employees would be given enough time to get trained in computer operation.

There are many styles of decision making and a leader has to adopt a suitable style of decision making depending upon the situation. The leader has to convince himself/herself that the decision he has taken is more rational than the next best alternative. The leader must be armed with all the facts and figures regarding the decision taken. Only then, he/she will be able to convince others on the importance of a particular decision taken. The problem and the solution forming part of the decision must be well structured so as to show how effective the decision will be. Then the leader has to decide whether the acceptance of the decision by the group is necessary or not. For example, the decision to air-condition the registered office need not be discussed with the factory workers. The leader also has to decide to what extent a decision is related to the goals and objectives of the organization.

In an organization, a leader may be called by different designations/titles. In each function, the leadership style changes according to the demands of job concerned.

How effective can a leader be? The effectiveness depends on the style of functioning a leader chooses — as an executive, developer, benevolent autocrat or as a well-meaning bureaucrat. Whatever role he/she may take, he/she has to function effectively. An executive concentrates both on the work and the people involved in the work to the maximum extent. A developer allocates more time for the people than the work. According to him/her, the work gets accomplished automatically if the people are taken care of. A benevolent dictator gives more importance for the work than the people. In his/her view, if the production is more, the workers will get their due incentive and get satisfied. A bureaucrat wants to carry on the administration by the rules and consequently he/she will not be popular among the workers.

Certain types of leaders prove themselves to be ineffective. For example, a compromiser will be ineffective since he/she will not be able to take quick decisions. A missionary will be too much inclined in favour of the workers and consequently his/her attention toward the work will suffer. An autocrat will never be liked by the workers and so his/her methods may not always work.

Sanskrit Sources on Leadership

When we talk of an ideal leader, the first person who comes to our mind is Śrī Rāma. His characteristics are enlisted in the first chapter of the *Vālmīki Rāmāyaṇa*. Some of them refer to his inner personality and some, his external charisma like lustre, broad shoulders, long arms, broad chest, attractive cheeks, neck, forehead, big eyes and so on. The poet begins by calling him *niyatātmā* one who has controlled the self. The self is indicated by the term "I" in ordinary speech. In other words, it is the centre of ego. The feeling of "I" is inevitable since it is the very basis of existence and consciousness. Only a conscious person will have the feelings such as "I am here" or "I am doing this." But the feeling of "I" should be subdued. Any undue importance given to it leads to selfishness and egoism that are the root cause for majority of interpersonal problems. Rāma demonstrated by his own example how one should control the ego. It is very well brought out by Kālidāsa in his *Raghuvaṁśa*.

दधतो मङ्गलक्षौमे वसानस्य च वल्कले।
ददृशुर्विस्मितास्तस्य मुखरागं समं जनाः।।

dadhato maṅgalakṣaume vasānasya ca valkale ।
dadṛśuḥ vismitā tasya mukharāgaṁ samaṁ janāḥ ।।
— *Raghuvaṁśa*, XII.8

When he wore the silken garments fit for the coronation and also when he wore the bark garments fit for the forest life (a few hours later) his facial expression remained the same and seeing that, the people were struck with wonder.

Vālmīki further speaks of Rāma's courage, heroic qualities, wisdom, unbiased nature, equanimity, virtue, and adherence to truth. Then he emphasizes the importance of the control of one's sense organs, which is exemplified by Rāma's indifference to the enticement of Śūrpanakhā. Another epithet that eulogizes Rāma is *adīnātmā*, that is, "not considering oneself as miserable." The *Bhagavad-Gītā* is very specific in saying that one should never underestimate oneself.

उद्धरेदात्मानात्मानं नात्मानमवसादयेत्।
आत्मैव ह्यात्मनो बन्धुरात्मैव रिपुरात्मनः रिपुः।।

uddharedātmānātmānaṁ nātmānamavasādayet ।
ātmaiva hyātmano bandhur ātmaiva ripurātmanaḥ ripuḥ ।।
— *Bhagavad-Gītā*, VI.5

One should elevate oneself by one's own efforts and one should never downgrade oneself; for, one's own self is the best relative (of oneself); one's own self is also the worst enemy (of oneself).

Rāma is *sarvalokapriyaḥ* one who is liked by the entire world. It may be difficult to please everybody at the same time. But one can desist from incurring the wrath of others. Another hallmark of a leader is accessibility. Vālmīki says that Rāma was approached by all the noble souls like the ocean being resorted to by the rivers. He was deep like the ocean, upright like the Himalayas, heroic like Lord Viṣṇu, pleasing to look at like the moon; in his anger towards the wicked, he was like the cosmic fire; in forbearance he was like the earth; in sacrifice, he was like Kubera, in his adherence to truth, he was verily Dharma.

At the death of Rāvaṇa, Vibhīṣaṇa abuses him. Rāma stops him and says: "No, Vibhīṣaṇa, Rāvaṇa was a great warrior. He was a great king. All enmities end with the death of a person. Perform his funeral rites."

A leader must be aware of ups and downs in life. He/She should take them in his/her stride. He/She should not over rejoice at prosperity nor breakdown at adversity. The *Rāmāyaṇa* (II.105-06) says:

सर्वे क्षयान्ता निचया: पतनान्ता: समुच्छ्र्या:।
सम्योगा विप्रयोगान्ता: मरणान्तं तु जीवितम्।।

sarve kṣayāntā nicayāḥ patanāntāḥ samucchrayāḥ।
samyogā viprayogantāḥ maraṇāntaṁ tu jīvitam।।

All accumulations come to an end by depletion. Elevations end by crumbling and falling. Unions end in separation. Life itself ends by death.

Sanskrit rhetoricians emphasize the importance of a good hero for the literary works, since they will be taken as role models by the public. Daṇḍin says:

आदिराजयशोबिम्बमादर्शं प्राप्य वाङ्मयम्।
तेषामसन्निधानेऽपि न स्वयं पश्य नश्यति।।

ādirājayaśobimbamādarśaṁ prāpya vāṅmayam।
teṣāmasannidhāne 'pi na svayaṁ paśya naśyati॥
— *Kāvyādarśa*, I.3

Just behold, the entire disc of the fame of the great kings of the yore, having got the mirror of literary works, do not perish, even though they themselves (the kings) have perished.

A mirror reflects an object as far as it is within its range. But the mirror of literary works continues to reflect the glories of leaders, who have moved out of the reach of the mirror itself (their demise).

The Rhetorical works list out qualities expected of a leader (hero). They are:

(i) Nobility of birth,
(ii) Personal charisma,
(iii) Prosperity,
(iv) Magnanimity,
(v) Fame,
(vi) Enterprising nature, and
(vii) Adherence to *dharma*

Pratāparudrīya explains the last one with this illustration:

परिहासेऽप्यनौचित्यं स्वप्नेऽप्यन्यवधूकथा।
शत्रावप्यगुणारोपं काकतीन्द्रो न मृष्यति॥

parihāse 'pyanaucityaṁ svapne 'pyanyavadhūkathā।
śatrāvapyaguṇāropaṁ kākatīndro na mṛṣyati॥
— I.31

Propriety even in making fun, avoidance of gossip relating to women even in dream and not finding fault even in an enemy — these are the marks of noble man.

In the first canto of *Raghuvaṁśa*, Kālidāsa gives an idea about leadership qualities when he speaks of the kings of the Raghu dynasty:

यथाविधिहुताग्नीनां यथाकामार्चितार्थिनाम्।
यथापराधदण्डानां यथाकालप्रबोधिनाम्॥

yathāvidhihutāgnīnāṁ yathākāmārcitārthinām।
yathāparādhadaṇḍānāṁ yathākālaprabodhinām॥
— *Raghuvaṁśa*, I.6

The kings performed the rituals as per the scriptures, honoured the suppliants as they liked and enforced punishment on the punishable in relation to the offence committed and updated themselves in knowledge as needed from time to time.

त्यागाय संभृतार्थानां सत्याय मितभाषिणाम्।
यशसे विजिगीवूणां प्रजायै गृहमेधिनाम्॥

tyāgāya sambhṛtārthānāṁ satyāya mitabhāṣiṇām।
yaśase vijigīvūṇāṁ prajāyai gṛhamedhinām॥
— Ibid., I.7

They earned only to spend it for useful purposes. They spoke little while upholding truth (if one speaks much, one is likely to utter some untruth). They conquered enemies only for fame (not for subjugating them).

ज्ञाने मौनं क्षमा शक्तौ त्यागे श्लाघाविपर्ययः।
गुणा गुणानुबन्धित्वात्तस्य सप्रसवा इव॥

jñāne maunaṁ kṣamā śaktau tyāge ślāghāviparyayaḥ।
guṇā guṇānubandhitvāttasya saprasavā iva॥
— Ibid., I.22

Holding silence notwithstanding full knowledge of things, forgiveness in spite of strength (to punish), munificence without desire to praise — though apparently opposite to each other, these qualities found a happy blend in Dilīpa.

प्रजानां विनयाधानाद्रक्षणाद्भरणादपि।
स पिता पितरस्तासां केवलं जन्महेतवः॥

prajānāṁ vinayādhānādrakṣaṇādbharaṇādapi।
sa pitā pitarastāsāṁ kevalaṁ janmahetavaḥ।

— Ibid., I. 24

On account of imparting moral training, on account of giving protection and on account of supporting his subjects, he was their father; while their actual fathers were mere authors of their coming to the earth.

द्वेष्योऽपि संमतः शिष्टस्तस्यार्तस्य यथौषधम्।
त्याज्यो दुष्टः प्रियोऽप्यासीदङ्गुलीवोरगक्षता॥

dveṣyo 'pi saṁmataḥ śiṣṭastasyārtasya yathauṣadham।
tyājyo duṣṭaḥ priyo 'pyāsīdaṅgulīvor gakṣatā॥

— Ibid., I.28

A righteous person, even if he were to be an enemy, was liked by him (Dilīpa) just as medicine is welcomed by a sick man; a wicked person even though endearing was discarded by him like a finger bitten by a cobra.

The *Vidura-Nīti* prescribes a number of qualities for a wise man which are applicable to a leader as well.

आत्मज्ञानं समारम्भस्तितिक्षा धर्मनित्यता।
यमर्थात् नापकर्षन्ति स वै पण्डित उच्यते॥

ātmajñānaṁ samārambhas titikṣā dharma nityatā।
yamarthāt na apakarṣanti sa vai paṇḍita ucyate॥

— *Vidura-Nīti* I.21

He is a wise man whom knowledge of the self, exertion, forbearance and steadfastness of virtue do not drag away from the goals of life.

निषेवते प्रशस्तानि निन्दितानि न सेवते।
अनास्तिकः श्रद्धधान एतत् पण्डितलक्षणम्।।

niṣevate praśastāni ninditāni na sevate।
anāstikaḥ śraddhadhāna etat paṇḍitalakṣaṇam।।

— Ibid., I.23

Attachment to the laudable, rejection of the blamable, belief in God and reverence to elders — these are the qualities of a wise man.

क्रोधो हर्षश्च दर्पश्च ह्री स्तंभो मान्यमानिता।
यमर्थान्नापकर्षन्ति स वै पण्डित उच्यते।।

krodho harṣaśca darpaśca hrī staṁbho mānyamānitā।
yamarthānnāpakarṣanti sa vai paṇḍita ucyate।।

— Ibid., I.24

He whom neither anger nor joy, neither pride nor bashfulness, neither obstinacy (rigidity) nor self-esteem, drags away from the high ends of life (is a wise man).

यस्य कृत्यं न जानन्ति मन्त्रं वा मन्त्रिते परे।
कृतमेवास्य जानन्ति स वै पण्डित उच्यते।।

yasya kṛtyaṁ na jānanti mantraṁ vā mantrite pare।
kṛtamevāsya jānanti sa vai paṇḍita ucyate।।

— Ibid., I.25

He whose proposed action, policy or resolution, others do not know of beforehand, but only after they are carried out is a wise man.

यथाशक्तिचिकीर्षन्ति यथाशक्ति च कुर्वते।
न किञ्चिदवमन्यन्ते नराः पण्डितबुद्धयः।।

yathāśakti cikīrṣanti yathāśakti ca kurvate।
na kiñcidavamanyante narāḥ paṇḍitabuddhayaḥ।।

— Ibid., I.28

> Those are wise men who aspire to do as much as lies in their power, do act to the best of their ability and do not look down upon anything.

The foremost characteristic of a wise man is that he understands concepts quickly, listens to others patiently, grasps the main purport and applies it judiciously. He does not spend his energy in the affairs of others, unasked.[2]

> नाप्राप्यमभिवाञ्छन्ति नष्टं नेच्छन्ति शोचितुम्।
> आपत्सु न च मुह्यन्ति नराः पण्डितबुद्धयः।।
> *nāprāpyamabhivāñchanti naṣṭam necchanti śocitum।*
> *āpatsu na ca muhyanti narāḥ paṇḍitabuddhayaḥ।।*
> — Ibid., I.30

> A wise man undertakes the task after due consideration, who, once begun, does not stop in the middle of his action, who never wastes his time and who has his mind under control.

Other characteristics of a leader that are stated in the text are:[3]

(i) They are devoted to noble deeds,

(ii) They are engaged in actions that lead to prosperity,

(iii) They are never jealous of others,

(iv) They do not over-rejoice on the honours conferred on them,

(v) They are eloquent, can see pros and cons of things and one endowed with ready insight into every rising problem and who can quote the authority quickly and interpret them, and

---

2. I.29, also quoted in chapter 3, p. 49

3. See 'पण्डितलक्षणम्' in *Vidura-Nīti*, chapter 1.

(vi) He should avoid sleep, drowsiness, fear, anger, laziness and procrastination.

Bhāravi, in his *Kirātārjunīya*, brings out some of the leadership qualities:

समवृत्तिरुपैति मार्दवं समये यश्च तनोति तिग्मताम्।
अधितिष्ठति लोकमोजसा स विवस्वानिव मेदिनीपतिः॥

samavṛttirupaiti mārdavaṁ samaye yaśca tanoti tigmatām।
adhitiṣthati lokamojasā sa vivasvāniva medinīpatiḥ॥
— *Kirātārjunīya*, II.38

That king who maintains an even course of conduct and assumes mildness or displays severity at the proper time, presides over the whole world, like the sun by his lustre.

Leaders have their own followers who are prepared to die for them. It is the responsibility of the leaders to direct the efforts of such faithful followers towards constructive activities. When a leader instigates his/her followers to destroy or cause damage to something they will do it immediately. A leader must realize that while destruction is easier, growth takes a long time. A coconut tree may take 25 years to attain its full growth but it can be cut down in an hour's time. A leader has to inspire his/her team members for the overall growth of the organization. He/She has to build a team and guide the team members towards organizational goals, which is taken up for discussion in chapter 7.

7

Team Building

Definition of a Team

A TEAM is defined as a cluster of two or more people who interact and influence each other towards a common purpose.[1]

At least two persons are required to form a team. Sometimes newspaper columns refer to one-man demolition squad, for example, in cricket, when a single person contributes heavily with both bat and ball to defeat an opponent. The expression is used only in a figurative sense to eulogize the extraordinary feat of an individual in a team. Though the definition does not prescribe any upper limit, in practice, a team has a maximum of about 20 members. If it is larger than this, it is called a contingent rather than a team.

If a team has more than 40 or 50 members, it will become a crowd and it becomes increasingly difficult to control such a large group. The next point in the definition makes it clear. A team is one where a lot of interaction takes place, which is not possible in a large crowd. A team has to meet and the members have interaction among themselves. It is not a classroom where a teacher does the maximum talking and the students are expected to listen. In a team meeting, the team leader acts only as a facilitator. The team members freely discuss the agenda. They not only put forth their own point, but also

1. Stoner, J.A.F., R.E. Freedom and D.R. Gilbert, p. 699.

comment on the views expressed by others without any fear or favour. This brings in a sense of responsibility in the arguments put forth by the team members. They must put across valid arguments and substantiate them so that they are accepted by the team members. Hence we have the term "influencing each other" in the definition. In such a discussion, the focus should not be lost. The discussions should not go off the track and if it does, the team leader has to bring it back to the main point of discussion. The efforts of the team, either at the discussion stage or at the implementation stage, should be oriented toward organizational goal. Only then, the purpose of forming the team will be served.

Types of Teams

Traditionally, two types of teams existed in organizations; formal and informal. In the present-day context, the gap between the two types has narrowed down and so the teams have the features of both.

Formal teams are created by the managements in order to carry out specific tasks to achieve the organizational goals. The most common formal teams are production team, sales team, purchase team, etc. The respective managers and people under them form such teams, which are more or less permanent though members may change on account of retirement etc.

Some formal teams are temporary and are formed only for a specific purpose. They are called task forces or protect teams. Once the project is over, the team will be dissolved. For example, teams are formed at each polling booth during elections. After the elections are over, they go back to their respective offices.

Informal teams are formed whenever people come together and interact regularly among themselves. For example, some members of an organization interested in football may assemble on the ground everyday after office hours and play a match or two. There are certain advantages in an informal team. It caters to the common interest of the members. Further, it creates a feeling of satisfaction among the employees who otherwise do their routine work in the office and get exhausted. For example, an employee may get the feeling, "I am only a clerk in the office, carrying out the orders of the manager. But here, on the football ground, I am the king." The informal activities help to develop friendship, support and security among the team members.

The third point is that the informal group members communicate among themselves in a better fashion than the formal group members on account of a tension-free environment in which they meet.

The fourth advantage is that members of the informal team solve their problems with the help of other members of the team who have similar interests.

Other Types of Teams

HIGH-PERFORMANCE TEAM

In the present-day scenario, when we talk about workers' participation in managements, teams are formed consisting of the characteristics of both formal and informal teams. With the advancement of media communications and technology, sweeping changes have come up in advertisement industry. When a company wants to come out with an advertisement, it forms a high-performance team. The team may consist of just one or two members from the company. The other members of the team would be the director of the film, script writer, camera person, music director, art director, editor, and so on.

The aim of the entire team would be to bring out a lively advertisement that would catch the imagination of the viewers; in short, towards a high performance.

SELF-MANAGED TEAMS

Self-managed teams have come to stay particularly in the software and IT industry. Such teams function without any formal supervision and direction. They have the responsibility for the entire task. The team decides its own work, methods, time schedule and assignments to team members.

OUTSOURCING TEAM

A big company with its heavy overhead expenditure may outsource the manufacture of certain components through smaller teams. It may work out cheaper for the company.

Characteristics of the Team

Generally, teams move through five stages: formation stage, discussion stage, documentation stage, performance stage and concluding stage. In the first stage, a team is formed and the team members are apprised of the purpose for which the team is formed. They are told about the task on hand. In this stage, team members acclimatize themselves to the new environment and get to know each other. In the discussion stage, brainstorming sessions are held and the methodology to be adopted for completing the task is discussed. In the third stage, the outcome of the discussions are documented and the norms are evolved. Rules and regulations are formed. In the performance stage, the team members plunge into action and begin to operate as one unit. The fruits of the endeavours begin to appear in this stage. In the concluding stage, the team wraps up its activities and perhaps gets ready to be disbanded. Reports are submitted, finished products are presented and the team gets rewarded for its efforts.

Team Cohesiveness

The solidarity or cohesiveness of a team is an important indicator of how much influence the group has over its individual members. The more cohesive the team, the more is the sense of belongingness of the team members. The cohesiveness introduces healthy competition between the members and between the different teams. The teams vie with each other in completing the task within the stipulated time. The cohesiveness among the members of the team strengthens interpersonal relationship between them. Each one tries to supplement and complement the other in accomplishing the task. The slow performers are offered a helping hand and encouraged to show improved performance. The cohesiveness contributes to increased interaction among the members leading to comradeship and integrity.

Sanskrit Sources on Team Building

The *Ṛgveda* sets the tone for team building in its immortal statement,

> संगच्छध्वं संवदध्वं संवो मनांसि जानताम्।
> *saṅgacchadhvaṁ saṁvadadhvaṁ saṁ vo manāṁsi jānatām*।
> — *Ṛgveda* X.19.2

> Let us work as a team marching together, speaking in one voice and united in mind.

The *Taittirīya Upaniṣad* (2.1.1) advocates team spirit between the teacher and the taught.

> सह नाववतु सह नौ भुनक्तु सह वीर्यं करवावहै।
> तेजस्विनावधीतमस्तु मा विद्विषावहै।।
>
> *saha nāvavatu saha nau bhunaktu saha vīryaṁ karavāvahai*।
> *tejasvināvadhītamastu mā vidviṣāvahai*।।

May the eternal guard us both
May the eternal rule us both
May we both make a bold attempt
May our studies become illuminative
May no difference arise between us

The Vedic seers visualized a team consisting of not only human beings but also birds and animals. The prayers are meant for common welfare of the entire community.

ओं तच्छं योरावृणीमहे।
गातुं यज्ञाय।
गातुं यज्ञपतये।
दैवी स्वस्तिरस्तु नः।
स्वस्तिर्मानुषेभ्यः।
ऊर्ध्वं जिगातु भेषजम्।
शंनोऽस्तु द्विपदे।
शं चतुष्पदे।
ओं शान्तिः शान्तिः शान्तिः॥

oṁ tacchaṁ yorāvṛṇīmahe ।
gātuṁ yajñāya ।
gātuṁ yajñapataye ।
daivī svastirastu naḥ ।
svastirmānuṣebhyaḥ ।
ūrdhvaṁ jigātu bheṣajam ।
śaṁ no astu dvipade ।
śaṁ catuṣpade ।
om śāntiḥ śāntiḥ śāntiḥ ॥

— *Śānti mantra*

We pray for that which shall remove all our ills
We pray for a proper direction in our worship
We pray for the worshipper

May we have the real divine!
May all men be happy!
May their ills be cured more and more!
May the birds be happy
May the animals be happy.
In the name of the eternal, may there be peace, peace and peace everywhere.

One of the important characteristics of Rāma is his ability to build a team. He first builds a team with his own brothers; he puts Bharata in-charge of the kingdom and leads his own team consisting of Lakṣmaṇa and Sītā to the forest. The team building *guru* for Rāma is none other than sage Viśvāmitra himself. He asks Daśaratha for not only his eldest son but the team of both Rāma and Lakṣmaṇa for the task of protecting his own *yajña* from the demons. On the way to the forest, the sage teaches them the use of a number of missiles. The two blast away all the demons and protect the sacrifice.

Lakṣmaṇa is known for his impetuosity and anger. As a team leader Rāma kept him under check always. Likewise, when Rāma is short of confidence after the abduction of Sītā, it is Lakṣmaṇa who revives his spirit with his encouraging words. "We shall kill Rāvaṇa and redeem Sītā. You should not thus despair. How can you let weakness come over you? If we lose a precious thing we should work for its recovery with perseverance. Sometimes very affection of ours becomes our enemy. Too much of love brings on grief and grief weakens effort. Let us forget grief and bend our mind and body to exertion. Be brave. Be hopeful. Get rid of your grief. We shall succeed." What a wonderful team man Lakṣmaṇa is!

True to the Vedic statement quoted earlier, Rāma builds a team with birds and animals. He befriends Sugrīva and Āñjaneya after Sītā's abduction. Sugrīva was in a similar state as Rāma. He was also leading a life of exile from the kingdom and he was also separated from his wife.

Generally, a team will succeed if the members are in a similar condition, for example, in a company, the newly recruited members are in a similar condition. All of them want to prove themselves and establish themselves. If they do not succeed, they may lose their job. So they work day and night and finish their project.

So, Hanumān helps Rāma and Sugrīva to form a team. The agreement is that Rāma would kill Vāli and make Sugrīva the king of the Vānara kingdom and Sugrīva would help Rāma in recovering Sītā. They swore by mutual friendship. "Let us share our joys and sorrows. Let our friendship be eternal." Sugrīva also encourages Rāma by saying, "Do not yield to grief that weakens the spirit. Look at me, I have controlled my sorrows and keep my courage up. If a *vānara* can do this, it should be easier for you to do the same. I beg you to control your grief and be brave." Rāma regains his composure and says, "I shall make your cause mine and make you the king again. I have never uttered a vain or false word in my life and never will. Tell me frankly how I can bring you relief. I shall do it."

Rāma keeps his promise and so does Sugrīva. Rāma adds to his team, Vibhīṣaṇa also, allaying the fears of Sugrīva and others. The team looked vulnerable before the mighty army of Rāvaṇa. But Rāma's team was high in spirits. Their unconventional warefare upset the rhythm of the *rākṣasas* who were finally subjugated and vanquished. It proves the point that innovation combined with team spirit can bring laurels. More than the number of persons in a team, it is the quality of work and the confidence level that matter most.

The same point is emphasized in the *Mahābhārata* also. The Kaurava army was nearly one and a half times larger than the Pāṇḍava army in numerical strength. But they were defeated.

The reason was that the leaders of the Kaurava army had mutual suspicion about one another. Duryodhana suspected that Bhīṣma had a soft corner for the Pāṇḍavas. Karṇa incurred the displeasure of everybody by his sharp tongue. Droṇa did have a special attachment for Arjuna and also had excessive attachment to his own son Aśvatthāmā. The Pāṇḍavas had the advantage of the Lord Kṛṣṇa's support, which proved vital in their success.

The *Pañcatantra* and the *Hitopadeśa* emphasize the importance of team building through didactic fables. The *Hitopadeśa* says:

अल्पानामपि वस्तूनां संहतिः कार्यसाधिका।
तृणैः गुणवन्तमापन्नैः बध्यन्ते मत्तदन्तिनः॥

alpānāmapi vastūnāṁ saṁhatiḥ kāryasādhikā।
tṛṇaiḥ guṇavantamāpannaiḥ badhyante mattadantinaḥ॥

— *Hitopadeśa*, I.35

Even ordinary people lacking in expertise will succeed if they form a team with like-minded people. An illustration is set forth here. Wild elephants are tied down by means of dry grass twisted into a rope.

True to the statement "charity begins at home," team building should start first at the family level. One should have a firm bondage with the members of the family who know each other from close quarters and who are aware of each other's strengths and capabilities.

संहतिश्च श्रेयसी पुंसां स्वकुलैरल्पकैरपि।
तुषेनापि परित्यक्ता न प्ररोहन्ति तण्डुलाः॥

saṁhatiśca śreyasī puṁsāṁ svakulairalpakairapi।
tuṣeṇāpi parityaktā na prarohanti taṇḍulāḥ॥
— Ibid., I.36

In a family, every member, small or big is equally important, so in a team. Rice, stripped of its husk will not grow.

We have an interesting story in the *Hitopadeśa* that brings about the importance of team spirit. Some birds were caught in a net cast by a hunter. Reminding themselves of team spirit, they all flew together carrying off the net. One of them had a friend in a mouse. They went near its place. The mouse was happy to welcome its friend but was shocked to see it being caught in the net. It started cutting the net with its sharp teeth. But the bird stopped him and said, "Friend, first cut the bonds of my followers and then you will cut mine." This is team spirit.

What are the qualities expected of team members? The *Hitopadeśa* says:

शुचित्वं त्यागिता शौर्यं सामान्यं सुखदुःखयोः।
ताक्षिण्यं चानुरक्तिश्च सत्यता च सुहृद्गुणाः।

śucitvaṁ tyāgitā śauryaṁ sāmānyaṁ sukhaduḥkhayoḥ।
tākṣiṇyaṁ ca anuraktiśca satyatā ca suhṛdguṇāḥ॥[2]
— *Hitopadeśa*, I.102

Purity of purpose, generosity, courage, sameness of behaviour in pleasure or pain, politeness, affection and truthfulness are the characteristics of friends forming a team.

Hitopadeśa also points out the possible faults that can spoil a team. They are:

रहस्यभेदो याञ्छा च नैष्ठूर्यं चलचित्तता।
क्रोधो निस्सत्यता द्यूतमेतत् मित्रस्य दूषणम्॥

2. Also quoted in *Kāmandakīya Nīti*, verse 4075.

rahasyabhedo yāñchā ca naiṣṭūryaṁ calacittatā ।
krodho nissatyatā dyūtametat mitrasya dūṣaṇam ॥
— *Hitopadeśa*, I.98

Divulging a secret, begging, hard heartedness, fickleness of mind, anger, faithlessness and gambling are the faults of friendship.

We have seen five stages of team development. One is struck by the similarity of these five stages to the five stages of development of a plot as prescribed by the Sanskrit dramaturgical texts.

The dramatic action is divided into five stages — commencement (*ārambha*), endeavour (*yatna*), prospect of success (*prāptyāśā*), certainty of success (*niyatāpati*) and consummation (*phalāgama*).

In the first one (commencement), the stage of action reveals the inclination and zeal of the principal hero to achieve the object of his desire. As the will precedes all action, it is the expression of a will and an effective thrust that pervades the first course of dramatic action. The second stage (endeavour) covers the expression of anxiety, which is a mental phenomenon, and it propels the hero to find and try all possible means to achieve the end.

In the third stage (prospect of success), there is hope of hitting the mark though it is beset with problems and chances of missing the ultimate goal.

In the fourth stage, all impediments that stand in the way of begetting success are removed.

In the last stage, all dramatic actions converge at the grand finale. The hero is crowned with success and the message is conveyed emphatically.

Collateral with the five stages of action, we have the five elements of the plot. They represent the dramatic action subjectively while the five stages present the same objectively. The elements are: the germ (*bīja*), the drop (*bindu*), the episode (*patākā*), the incident (*prakarī*) and the denouement (*kārya*).

The germ represents the seed of dramatic action. For example, Duṣyanta's attraction for Śakuntalā at the first sight may be called the seed of the entire drama.

The *bindu* is like a drop of oil that falls on a sheet of water and spreads. The main plot of the story slowly unfolds itself here. It is the cause of resuming the main purpose of the play, which has got interrupted for a while. For example, after the first meeting with Śakuntalā, Duṣyanta has to divert his attention towards the protection of the sacrifice conducted by the sages. When everything calms down, he meets Śakuntalā again and their mutual love reaches a high point.

The third element, *patākā* is a fairly long narrative that is woven within the main plot. We find a lot of such narratives in the dramas dealing with the *Rāmāyaṇa* and the *Mahābhārata* stories (e.g. Bhagīratha story and Hariścandra story).

The fourth element is an "incident," that is connected to the main story. For example, the Durvāsā episode and the curse that Duṣyanta would forget Śakuntalā is an "incident." Consequently, Duṣyanta refuses to accept Śakuntalā as his wife.

The fifth element of the plot is the denouement, which depicts the cause or the motif of the play. The desired goal is achieved in this. For example, the happy reunion of Duṣyanta and Śakuntalā takes place in the denouement of the play.

Sanskrit dramaturgical writers have identified five "junctures" (*sandhis*) which are component divisions of the dramatic action. The first one is called *mukha sandhi,* which is comparable to the Protasis of the Greek Drama. The first stage of action (commencement) and the first element of the plot (germ) combine to form the *mukha sandhi*. In this *sandhi,* a variety of characters, incidents and sentiments are introduced. It will be interesting to note how several portions of the dramatic action are developed in Kālidāsa's *Abhijñāna-śākuntalam* in the *mukha sandhi.*

(i) The hero suggests the germ of action or makes a mention of what he wants to achieve. Duṣyanta, being fascinated by the natural beauty of Śakuntalā says (he was to say this to his friend later) "She is an un-smelt flower, a delicate shoot not touched by hand, a raw uncut diamond, fresh honey that is not tasted by anybody or the full reward of meritorious deeds. I know not whom destiny has chosen as her husband." His desire to marry her is suggested here.

(ii) Some likely impediments are sorted out. Duṣyanta wonders whether Śakuntalā is destined to remain a life-long ascetic. Her friends make it clear that she is to be given away in marriage.

(iii) Duṣyanta has a doubt whether Śakuntalā is interested in him. Her longing look at the king, under the pretext of taking out the thorn from her foot suggests that she is also favourably inclined towards him.

In the *pratimukha sandhi* (progression) the germ that has gained ground is sprouted, as it were, but is visible only partially. For example, in the second act of *Śākuntalam,* the king decides to stay back in the vicinity of the hermitage for a few days on the request of the hermits. He has an overwhelming desire to see Śakuntalā again and express his love to her. He also tells his friend that the Śakuntalā episode is not to be taken seriously and that it was only a light-hearted affair. These words have a bearing on the plot in Act V.

The third *sandhi* is called *garbha sandhi* and it is equivalent to Catastasis of the Greek drama. Here the seed of the plot grows further but hindrances arise. The main event plays hide and seek. The curiosity of the spectators is kept alive and the suspense is heightened. For example, in *Śākuntalam*, Duṣyanta, hiding behind the bushes, sees his beloved writing a love letter to him. He shows himself up and takes her hand. He also presents her with the signet ring and goes back to his city with the promise that he will take her to his court with due honours.

After his departure, the sage Durvāsā visits the hermitage but Śakuntalā being engrossed in thoughts about her husband fails to take notice of his (sage's) visit. The sage pronounces a curse that her husband will forget her. Being requested by her friends, the sage shows a concession that on seeing the token of recognition, memories of Śakuntalā will come back to her husband.

The fourth *sandhi* is called *avamarśa sandhi* which is equivalent to Epitasis. This is the juncture when there is a grave danger to the core idea. In the play under discussion, the scene of Act V is an example for this. Śakuntalā is taken to the court of king Duṣyanta who refuses to accept her, since, according to him, he had never met her before (the effect of the sage's curse acts). This comes as a rude shock to the poor girl. She appeals to her mother, the celestial nymph Menakā who takes her away.

The last *sandhi* is called *nirvahaṇa sandhi*, in which the germ is fully developed and attains the fruition stage. All the ends are tied and the theme is complete. In the play under discussion, the chance meeting of Duṣyanta and his son and also the reunion of the hero and heroine are the high points of this juncture.

Thus we see that there is a lot of correspondence between the five stages of team development and the five stages of development of the plot in a Sanskrit drama. Drama is only an extension of real life. There are real life situations in a drama and there are dramatic incidents in real life as well. Shakespeare says that all the world is a stage and all men and women are its characters. It is no wonder that there is similarity between dramatic action and management action. A person who is well versed in the development of a plot in a drama will be equally proficient in developing and executing a plan in his/her official duty as well. Hence, an attempt is made here to relate the two, with particular reference to team development.

8

Planning

PLANNING is an age-old concept. The first planner is the Almighty God who has planned the origin and evolution of the entire universe. All the stars and the planets move according to a systematic plan which is so meticulously organized. All human endeavours are also based on planning. The ancient temples of India are a standing testimony to the amount of planning that has gone into their structure that has lasted for a thousand years and more.

Individual Planning and Organizational Planning

History speaks of the achievements of great personalities like Alexander the great, king Aśoka, Akbar and Napoleon, all of whom must have planned for their glorious tasks and executed them meticulously.

Planning is a thinking process, an organized foresight and vision based on fact and experience that is required for an intelligent action.[1] All plans arise in the mind at the first stage. They may be spelt out or written down at a later stage. Plans are always meant for the future. Nobody plans for what has happened already. Hence, an element of foresight is necessary for planning. Past actions, facts and experience may provide a base for future planning. At first, aims are visualized and then planning is done for realizing the goals. Some amount of

1. Alford and Beathy, *Management*, 1975.

planning is necessary even for a daily routine like taking a bath. But they are not included in what we call as "planning." A planning is necessary for an intelligent action and this is what we mean by the definition of the term. If a person wants to become a lawyer, he/she must get the necessary qualification. Then he/she must register at the bar and get practical training under a leading lawyer. He/She must acquire a good memory power as he/she has to remember law points and the sections. He/She must also acquire a good oratory skill to put forth his/her arguments in a convincing fashion. All these require years of planning.

An organization has to do a lot of planning to achieve its goals. Once targets to be achieved are specified, all the departments such as purchases, manufacturing and marketing are geared up to plan for achieving the targets in the specified time. An organization has to plan for both present as well as future changes in the organization on account of government's policies and legislation. Changes may take place in the field of technology, attitudes of the customers and strategies of the competitors. Planning has to be done to meet all such contingencies. Planning is necessary to meet challenges of time and place. Otherwise, challenges will remain as challenges and cripple an organization.

What is Planning?

Planning is defined as that function of a manager in which he decides in advance what he will do. It is a decision-making process of a special kind; its essence is futurity.[2] One more point could be added here. Planning bridges the gap between where we are and where we want to go.[3]

---

2. Haynes and Massie, *Essentials of Management*.
3. Koontz Harold and O'Donnell, *Essentials of Management*, p. 62.

As contrasted from routine actions which can be done mechnaically, planning requires the use of intellect for its development.[4] Planning is an intellectual process, the conscious determination of courses of action, the basing of decisions on purpose, facts and considered estimates.[5]

Planning is an intellectually demanding function. It is the process of thinking before an action. It is today's projection for tomorrow's activity.[6] Planning is a deliberate attempt to influence, to exploit, bring about and control the nature, decision, extent, speed and effects of change.[7] To plan is to produce a scheme for future action, to bring about specified results at a specified cost, in a specified period of time. Planners cannot control the future but they should attempt to identify and isolate the present actions and their results that can be expected to influence the future.[8] A crisis situation may arise any time in a company. A manager has to anticipate them and prepare the possible solutions in a systematic manner. He/She has to assess the company's strengths and weaknesses, seize the opportunities and be prepared to meet the threats. Planning is not simply an attempt to predict the future; it is also an attempt to control it. A manager cannot have a casual attitude by thinking "Let us cross the bridge when we come to it." He/She has to assess the situation and formulate a course of action that will be beneficial to the company in the long run.

Planning involves four questions (i) Where are we now?, (ii) Where do we want to be?, (iii) What is the difference

---

4. Afford and Beathy, *Management*, 1975.
5. Koontz and O'Donnell, *Essentials of Management*, p. 62.
6. Robert Albanese, *Management Toward Accountability and Performance*.
7. Cyril L. Hudson, p. 101.
8. V.S.P. Rao, and P.S. Narayana, p. 10.

between the current position and the position we want to be in?, and (iv) How can we get there from here?

A question may be raised here. In spite of careful planning, we come across unexpected problems, resulting in a total collapse of the plan. Such being the case, why should we spend our energy and time in planning? It must be understood that planning is not meant to eradicate crisis. For example, nobody can stop a natural calamity like tsunami. But one should be prepared for it so that its ill effects could be minimized. For example, public halls and offices are provided with fire extinguishers, for, in case of a fire accident somewhere, the extinguishers can be used to put out the fire. Planning lays foundation for disciplined thinking and helps in avoiding snap judgements and haphazard actions.[9] Managerial planning attempts to achieve a consistent, co-ordinated structure of operation, focused on desired ends. Without plans, actions become merely random activity, producing nothing but chaos.[10]

Characteristics of Planning

Planning is the foundation of management and is an essential exercise in management process. It provides direction, purpose and incentive to the organizational development and the management functions.

Planning is a continuous process. Drawing up a plan for a particular process alone is not enough. A manager has to plan and also see whether things are going according to the schedule. If there is a deviation, the plan has to be fine-tuned and adjusted. Thus it is a continuous ongoing process.

Planning is pervasive in the sense that it is required

9. L.A. Allen, *Professional Management*, p. 63.

10. Earnest C. Miller, *Objectives and Standards; An Approach to Planning and Control*.

at every stage in every department. Plans can be centralized or decentralized. Certain problems are common to all the departments and therefore, there could be a centralized plan for them. Apart from that, each department may have its own aims and objectives. In order to realize them, each department may have to devise its own plans which are decentralized.

Another aspect of planning is flexibility. No planning can be too rigid. Every department has to devise a plan and also make suitable adjustments in adopting it. It has to adapt itself to the changing needs and circumstances.

Planning is not just a checklist for an exercise; it is an orientation towards sustained action. It should be realistic and enforceable. It should be neither too easy nor impossible to achieve. Plans must be so devised as to be achievable. Plans must be communicated properly so that they are understood by those who are to accomplish them.

Planning expects unity of action and purpose in all the departments concerned so that the focus is not lost. For example, if the production department plans for reduced production and the sales department plans for increased sales (unless when the piled up stock is to be cleared), there will be confusion, shifting of focus and loss of efficiency. Hence, plans must be drawn up in a coordinated fashion and there should be a consensus on it. Plans must go with common objectives and goals.

Participation and involvement are necessary for any plan to succeed. Planning is not a magic carpet taking one to any place one likes. It is a concerted effort by all those concerned, from the chief manager to the lowest worker toward achieving the organizational objective. It is necessary, therefore, that every employee is informed about the plan and also the ways and means of achieving it.

Steps in Planning

Planning is a step by step process. It starts from identification of goals. For example, maintenance of quality and cost effectiveness may be a goal. Unless a goal is defined, a plan cannot be drawn.

The second step is the collection of information. When a plan is to be devised, it is necessary to collect all information regarding the resources, the current status of the company and the current trends in the market. For example, when a publishing company decides to bring out textbooks, it procures the syllabus from the university, identifies authors who can write the lessons and collects information regarding the number of students who are likely to buy the books.

The third step is developing alternative courses if the plans are found wanting or when they become unsuitable under changed circumstances. So a regular plan must always be followed by a contingency plan for emergency.

The fourth step is the development of sub-plans within a broader plan to take care of the finer details. For example, under a plan developed by the management, each department will have to break it into several smaller plans and bring them to manageable levels. Each sub-plan can be entrusted to a small group which can accomplish it.

Types of Planning

FORMAL AND INFORMAL PLANNING

A routine and regular planning is called a formal planning. It is documented and developed in a systematic fashion. A plan that is not documented or recorded but is conceived and developed in the mind of the planner is called informal planning.

OPERATIONAL PLANNING

Operational plans are devised for a particular issue and they are short-range plans or standing plans. Market plans, production plans and financial plans come under operational planning.

STRATEGIC PLANNING

Every company develops certain strategies to capture the market or increase its market share. They are generally long-range plans. Strategic planning involves mission statement, evaluating the strengths and weaknesses of competitors and forecasting the future development.

Benefits of Planning

(i) Planning provides proper direction to all the activities of the organization.

(ii) Planning provides a unifying framework in the functioning of an organization. It helps one to prioritize the work to be done. In other words, planning makes it easier to distinguish the important work from the less important ones. Under a plan, all the departments in an organization are able to co-ordinate well as a single unit.

(iii) Planning helps an organization to control its expenditure. It is helpful in cutting down the unproductive expenditure.

(iv) Planning helps a management to adjust itself to changing circumstances and needs. A well-planned approach is the very basis of decision making. It reduces risks, mistakes and unexpected expenditure. It helps in avoiding crisis management which is always very expensive and risky.

(v) Planning brings about a behavioural change in the attitude of employees. When a plan is devised, all the employees have to be informed about it for proper implementation. The opinion of all employees is to be sought for the success of the programme envisaged. In such an atmosphere, every employee thinks that the plan is his/her own and he/she contributes to the successful implementation of the plan. This brings about a healthy atmosphere in the organization.

(vi) Planning is an education. It contributes to better knowledge and better understanding of the problems and solutions.

Impediments to Planning

(i) There are certain managements, which think that planning is a wasteful exercise; such an attitude will put blocks in planning.

(ii) Lack of records, lack of participation, lack of specific objectives and incompetence of the planner will cause a setback to planning.

(iii) At the implementation stage, there could be lack of flexibility, inability to change according to situations, lack of motivation, lack of orientation towards action and lack of proper training to meet exigencies, all of which may spoil a plan.

(iv) Planning is a costly exercise. In order to avoid financial loss or crisis situation, alternative plans should be kept in store.

(v) External factors like government rules may also stand in the way of planning.

Principles of Effective Planning

(i) Accurate forecasting based on statistical methods.

(ii) Educating all those concerned about the plan and its implementation.

(iii) Developing a sound plan cutting down all possible risk factors.

(iv) Fitting the plan according to the situation.

(v) Being objective and optimistic in devising a plan and implementing it.

Sanskrit Sources on Planning

The importance of planning has been very well brought out by a Subhāṣita stanza from *Śārṅgadharapaddhati* (verse 1440) which says:

चिन्तनीया हि विपदामदावेव प्रतिक्रिया।
न कूपखननंयुक्तं प्रदीप्ते वह्निना गृहे।।

cintanīyā hi vipadāmādau eva pratikriyā।
na kūpakhananaṁ yuktaṁ pradīpte vanhinā gṛhe।।

One should plan for remedial measures even before one comes across calamities. Digging a well is not a proper step to be taken when the house in ablaze with fire.

Administrative plans should not be divulged to all and sundry. The *Vidura-Nīti* says:

यस्य कृत्यं न जानन्ति मन्त्रं वा मन्त्रिते परे।
कृतमेवास्य जानन्ति स वै पण्डित उच्यते।।

yasya kṛtyaṁ na jānanti mantram vā mantrite pare।
kṛtamevāsya jānanti sa vai paṇḍita ucyate।।

— I.30

A wise man's plans, action, policy or resolution are not made known to others beforehand but only after they are carried out.

निश्चित्य यः प्रक्रमते नान्तर्वसति कर्मणः।
अवन्ध्यकालो पश्यात्मा स वै पण्डित उच्येत।।

niścitya yaḥ prakramate nāntarvasati karmaṇaḥ।
avandhyakālo paśyātmā sa vai paṇḍita ucyate।।

— I.31

A wise man undertakes the tasks after due consideration and planning. Having taken up, he does not stop his endeavours in the middle and never wastes his time.

अनुबन्धानवेक्षेत सानुबन्धेषु कर्मसु।
सम्प्रधार्य च कुर्वीत सहसा न समाचरेत्।।

anubandhānavekṣeta sānubandheṣu karmasu।
sampradhārya ca kurvīta sahasā na samācaret।।

— II.8

The success of a plan depends on the ability of the doer, the nature of the plan and the purpose served by it. A plan may have several links and sub-plans.

The *Vidura-Nīti* says that one should consider all these factors before commencing an action. The pros and cons should be analysed before proceeding with the work.

The plan should be so devised that its benefits would accrue spontaneously like the fruits of a tree.

वनस्पतेरपक्वानि फलानि प्रचिनोति यः।
स नाप्नोति रसं तेभ्यो बीजं चास्य विनश्यति।।

vanaspaterapakvāni phalāni pracinoti yaḥ।
sa nāpnoti rasaṁ tebhyo bījaṁ cāsya vinaśyati।।

— II.15

> He who plucks unripe fruits from a tree does not obtain juice from them and the seeds of the tree are also destroyed.

The idea is that having planned something, one should wait for its results patiently. Hasty action will lead to the collapse of the plans. Explaining this further with the help of the same metaphor, the author says:

यस्तु पक्वमुपादत्ते काले परिणतं फलम्।
फलाद्रसं स लभते बीजाच्चैव फलं पुनः।।

yastu pakvamupādatte kāle pariṇataṁ phalam ।
phalādrasaṁ sa labhate bījaccaiva phalaṁ punaḥ ।।
— II.16

> He who plucks the ripe fruit duly grown in the proper season, obtains the juice from that fruit and also the seeds (which when sown and grown render fruits again).

Like a gardener, one should pluck flowers one by one and not cut the tree by the root like the charcoal-maker.

यथा मधु समादत्ते रक्षन् पुष्पाणि षट्पदः।
तद्वर्थान् मनुष्येश्च आदद्यादविहिंसया।।

yathā madhu samādatte rakṣan puṣpāṇi ṣaṭpadaḥ ।
tdvarthān manuṣyeśca ādadyādavihiṁsayā ।।

> As the bee gathers honey from the flowers yet protecting them (not destroying) so also should a king collect taxes from the subjects without doing harm to them.

In fact, all the plans of an administrator should be so designed as to derive benefits without causing much strain to the employees or any other stakeholder, for that matter.

Plans should be achievable. A person who indulges in unachievable plans wastes his energy, time and money.

प्रसादो निष्फलो यस्य क्रोधश्चापि निरर्थकः।
न तं भर्तारमिच्छन्ति षण्डं पतिमिव स्त्रियः॥

prasādo niṣphalo yasya krodhaścāpi nirarthakaḥ।
na taṁ bhartāramicchanti ṣaṇḍaṁ patimiva striyaḥ॥

— II.22

People do not like to have him as their leader who is ever intent on useless pursuits and plans, as women do not like to have eunuchs as their husbands.

सुपुष्पितस्स्यादफलः फलितः स्याद्दुरारुहः।
अपक्वः पक्वसङ्काशो न तु शीर्येत कर्हिचित्॥

supuṣpitassyādaphalaḥ phalitaḥ syāddurāruhaḥ।
apakvaḥ pakvasaṅkāśo na tu śīryeta karhicit॥

— II.25

All the plans that are laid may not bear fruit. Though not bearing fruits, a tree should be full of blossoms. Though possessing fruits, it should be difficult to climb. Though unripe, the fruit should appear to be ripe, but in no case should it wither away.

The metaphor needs some explanation. An administrator is compared to a tree here. People resort to such trees that bear fruits. Some trees may not bear fruits; yet they may be attractive on account of their flowers. The fruits should be hanging in high branches (if they are in low branches, others will pluck them and go away. The owner will be left with none). Though actually unripe they should appear to be ripe.

Likewise, a manager whose plans are working well, will be approached by all the team members. Even if his/her plans are not tangible, if he/she speaks sweetly, people will flock to him/her. He/She should not be very easily accessible lest people should take him/her lightly. Though immature, he/she should appear to be knowledgeable so that he/she can command respect. On the other hand, if he/she exposes his/her weaknesses, he/she will be discarded by everybody like a barren tree.

Plan of Sandhi

The *Arthaśāstra* describes the plan of action while entering *sandhi*, that is, a treaty.

Sandhi may be resorted to when our forces are depleted. At the same time, we should try to weaken the other party so that we will be able to hold an upper hand. On striking *sandhi* with a like-minded party, we must try to outwit our enemy and ruin his resources. While entering into a *sandhi* with the enemy himself, we should come to know of his weaknesses and strike him at the appropriate time. If the enemy is at war with somebody, we may try to prolong the war so that his economy will be ruined. We should have a secret pact with the enemy's allies and try to wean them away from him (7.1.32).

The *Arthaśāstra* suggests several contingency plans for a weak king if he were to be attacked by a stronger king (7.3.22-36).

He should quickly propose *sandhi* offering treasury, army, himself or territory. If he surrenders himself, it is known as *ātmāmiṣa sandhi* (one with himself as the prey). If the weak king offers his commander-in-chief or the prince as a hostage, it is called *puruṣāntara sandhi* (treaty through another person). The weak king may be forced to leave the country in a treaty called *adr̥ṣṭapuruṣa sandhi* (with persons unseen). It may be remembered that Napoleon was forced to go in exile (to Elba, an island on the Mediterranean) according to one of the treaties that he entered into. By far the best treaty for a weak king is a "golden treaty" in which he enters into matrimonial alliance with the superior king. A question may arise here; is there any planning worth its name if one were to surrender to a superior force, by offering himself, land, army or treasury? It is not; if one surrenders without entering into a treaty. There is planning in entering into a treaty with or without surrendering something to a superior force. A treaty is always a mutual contract. By striking a treaty, even a weak king imposes certain restrictions on the superior force. In course of time, the weaker king may be able to mobilize his forces and turn the table against an erstwhile superior king.

Two kings may enter into a treaty for colonizing an unsettled land. Of the two, he who plans and occupies a land possessed of excellence overreaches the other. A land abounding in water resources, cultivable fields, mines, material forests, land routes and water routes is preferable, says Kauṭilya

In his *Raghuvaṁśa*, Kālidāsa speaks of planning at several places. In the seventeenth canto be refers to king Aditi's administration, in which he says.

कातर्यं केवला नीतिः शौर्यं श्वापदचेष्टितम्।
अतः सिद्धिं समेताभ्यामुभाभ्यामन्वियेष सः।।

kātaryaṁ kevalā nītiḥ śauryaṁ śvāpadaceṣṭitam।
ataḥ siddhiṁ sametābhyāmubhābhyāmanviyeṣa saḥ।।

— XVII.47

Planning without courage is cowardice; mere processing without planning is equivalent to the acts of wild animals. Therefore he tried to attain success through the employment of both.

The verse implies that mere planning on paper is useless. One must have courage and boldness to implement the plans that have been designed. Likewise, raw aggression is not advisable; it will result in loss of life and heavy expenditure. Caution coupled with aggression should be the watchword for administrators. Strategies must be planned well in advance before launching an action plan.

Some plans need to be kept as a secret. If they are made public, there is a danger that the enemies may take advantage of them and spoil them. Aditi's plans came to light only after they had been carried out.

भव्यमुख्याः समारम्भाः प्रत्यवेक्ष्या निरत्ययाः।
गर्भशालिसधर्माणस्तस्य गूढं विपेचिरे॥

bhavyamukhyāḥ samārambhāḥ pratyavekṣyā niratyayāḥ।
garbhaśālisadharmāṇastasya gūḍhaṁ vipecire॥

— XVII.53

The poet gives an illustration here. The shape of the paddy is quite evident in the beginning stage itself, but the rice comes out only after it had grown to the full ripe stage.

It is always better for an administrator to adopt a middle course instead of taking extremes. Referring to Aditi, the poet says:

हीनान्यनुपकर्तृणि प्रवृद्धानि विकुर्वते।
तेन मध्यमशक्तीनि मित्राणि स्थापितान्यतः॥

hīnānyanupakartṝṇi pravṛddhāni vikurvate।
tena madhyamaśaktīni mitrāṇi sthāpitānyataḥ॥

— XVII.58

The weak will not be helpful (because of their incapacity). The strong will do only harm. The king (Aditi), therefore, kept his friends at a medium level (neither weak nor strong).

As for the finance of the state, Aditi saw to it that the treasury had sufficient revenue since it is only a strong treasury that beckons people. It is only the water-bearing clouds that attract the (mythical) *cātaka* birds.

Carelessness and forgetfulness are the two enemies of planning. Care and attention are essential aspects of planning. Māgha says in his *Śiśupālavadha* (II.80):

उपायमास्थितस्यापि नश्यन्त्यर्थाः प्रमाद्यतः।
हन्ति नोपशयस्थोऽपि शयालुर्मृगयुर्मृगान्॥

upāyamāsthitasyāpi naśyantyarthāḥ pramādyataḥ।
hanti nopaśayastho 'pi śayālur mṛgayurmṛgān॥

> One who is careless, though capable of adopting the right means, fails in his object. A hunter, though an expert, never kills any deer, if he is overtaken by sleep.

Intellect is the basis of planning. Māgha brings out this aspect in a beautiful way. A plan is to be guided by intellect but not influenced by passion. A man blinded by passion and prejudice may fail to see the intricacies of the plan. He may not be able to foresee the future or anticipate possible impediments or find solutions for them.

तीक्ष्णा नारुन्तदा बुद्धिः कर्म शान्तं प्रतापवत्।
नोपतापि मनः सोष्म वागेका वाग्मिनः सतः॥

tīkṣṇā nāruntadā buddhiḥ karma śāntaṁ pratāpavat।
nopatāpi manaḥ soṣma vāgekā vāgminaḥ sataḥ॥
— *Śiśupālavadha*, II.109

> The intellect of a righteous man is sharp yet it never cuts the vitals of others; his activities will be highly energetic, yet never influenced by passion; his heart is full of warmth, yet never causes pain to others; he has the gift of speech, yet he has but one speech (that is, truth).

There are many stories bringing out the essence of planning, in *Pañcatantra* and *Hitopadeśa*. For want of space they could not be discussed here. But a discerning reader will be able to see many stories that exemplify planning and administration in them.

9

Organizational Behaviour

AN organization is formed by a group of people though there may be difference with respect to their positions. There could be a CEO, managers, supervisors and workers, all of whom are important for the growth of an organization. Every individual has an impression about the other persons with whom he/she comes into contact. For the successful running of an organization, every manager has to understand the personality, behaviour, attitude, learning ability and a perception of the people working under him/her.

Personality

Personality may be defined as the characteristics of a person that determine his/her behaviour and his/her emotional state at different situations. The factors that determine the personality are (i) Biological factors, (ii) Cultural factors, (iii) Social factors, and (iv) Environmental factors.

Biological factors are controlled by heredity, brain development and physical features. It may be observed that some people get agitated even for small things. It may be due to high blood pressure which again might have been passed on to him/her by his/her parents. Due to lack of brain power some people react slowly to situations. People who are short and ugly develop an inferiority complex within themselves. This comes under physical features.

The cultural background of a person also determines his/her personality. For example, it may be quite natural for a Western girl to go for dating but, for an Indian girl it may be a cultural shock.

Social factors also contribute to the personality of a person. For example, a 20-year old boy in India is still dependent on his parents because of the social conditions, while a boy of similar age in the USA may be totally independent.

The environment in which a person is brought up largely contributes to his/her personality. Students coming from convent schools are able to converse freely and express their opinion frankly while students coming from rural background develop inhibitions and hesitate to express their opinion freely. This is due to the environment in which they are brought up.

Theories of Personality

A number of theories on personality have been enunciated by psychologists. A few of them may be highlighted here.

Sigmund Freud[1] has formulated a theory called intra-psychic theory. According to him, mind is controlled by three structures within itself called (i) the Id, (ii) the ego, and (iii) the superego. Id refers to all that is inherited and is present at the time of birth, as for example, the desire for pleasure and a dislike of pains. The ego develops in a child when it learns to distinguish between unreality and reality. As far as it is fed by the mother, the child thinks that food is automatic which is an unreal situation. When it is no more possible to get mother's milk, it learns that it has to wait till milk is mixed and given to it in a bottle. Ego is rational and logical and it is the bridge between the realities of the world and the demands of the Id. Superego represents noblest thoughts, ideas and

1. Sigmund Freud, p. 14.

feelings, acquired by a person from his/her parents, teachers, friends, religion, culture and organization. The ego may propel an action prompted by Id but the superego decides whether it is right or wrong. The Id demands food immediately since it cannot put up with hunger. Ego finds that there is no money and without money food cannot be got. Id thinks that the only way is to steal some money. But the Superego says that it is wrong to steal money. It is better to go without food. So, there is a conflict between Id and superego. The ego now thinks of seeking the help of a well-meaning person. The ego tries to bring about compromise between the Id and the Superego. Such a defense mechanism is responsible for aggression, repression, rationalization, reaction, projection and interjection.

According to Carl Jung,[2] the personality of a person is determined by his being either an introvert or an extrovert. Introverts are less sociable, withdrawn and absorbed in inner life. Extroverts are friendly, sociable, interactive and out-spoken.

Carl Roger[3] has developed a theory called "Self-Theory." It consists of three concepts, namely, the self, the organization and the development of the self. The self consists of all perceptions, ideals and values. It is characterized by the feeling "I" and "Mine." The organism is the locus of all experience. Development of the self relates to self-actualization or derivation of fulfilment.

In addition to these theories which are helpful in understanding the psychology of human behaviour, a manager may also do well to know certain factors that are common to all human beings and certain others that differ from person to person. Intelligence is common to all human beings though the level may vary. Similarly, the ability to distinguish between

2. Carl Jung, p. 156.

3. Carl Rogers, p. 200.

what is good and what is bad exists in everyone. It is a different matter if a person fails to make use of it. The ability to find a shortest route to a goal is also present in every human being. He can make tools and find out innovative techniques to achieve something with lesser strain. The ability to gain something from another's experience and build-up on it is another common feature that is found in all human begins.

There are certain differences among human beings like im-portance attached to actions, tolerance level, ability to concent-rate, memory power, power of observation and perseverance.

Attitudes

Attitude may be defined as a predisposition of the individual to evaluate some object in a favourable or an unfavourable manner.

Attitude influences behaviour of people and their performance in an organization. A manager is, therefore, expected to know the attitudes of the employees in order to manage effectively.

The structure of a person's attitude comprises of three vital components: affective, cognitive, and overt.

The affective component refers to the emotions associated with an attitude object. For example, cow is considered very sacred in India and therefore, beef eating is not popular even among non-vegetarians. The feelings such as like or dislike, good and bad, pleasure or pain are the results of the affective component.

The cognitive component represents the beliefs of a person about an attitude object. It may be based on a learning experience, rumour, misunderstanding or any other information. A person may be considered as intelligent or stupid, ethical or unethical, autocratic or democratic depending upon the inputs an observer has.

The overt component concerns with the behavioural aspect. A person may behave positively or negatively towards another person or object.

Attitudes are formed on account of experience, association, family background, peer groups and society.

Attitudes are not permanent; they can be changed. An efficient manager can study the attitudes of the employees and bring about an attitudinal change in the minds of the employees from negative to the positive, from destructive to constructive, from isolation to participation.

Learning

Learning can be defined as a relatively permanent change in behaviour that occurs as a result of experience or reinforced practice.[4]

People learn new behaviour through one or more of the four learning processes, namely, classical conditioning, operant conditioning, observational learning and cognitive learning.

Classical conditioning has been demonstrated by the Russian scientist Pavlov. A dog was shown a piece a meat and a bell was also rung at the same time. The dog produced saliva on seeing the meat. After a few days the bell alone was sounded. But remembering the meat, the dog produced saliva. It has been conditioned to the fact that the sounding of the bell meant the arrival of meat.

Operant conditioning is the behaviour that produces effects. Individuals respond when a reward is waiting. They

---

4. Fred Luthas, p. 281.

do not respond when no reward is available. They also do not respond when punishment is expected.

Observational learning occurs on account of observing the results of the behaviour of another person. On seeing X being rewarded for a particular job done by him, Y also performs a good job in the hope of getting a reward, or when X is punished for a misbehaviour Y desists from committing the mistake.

Cognitive learning is what students get in the classroom atmosphere.

Perception

Perception is the mechanism by which people come to know about their surrounding groups. It is a psychological process. By the power of perception, a manager will be able to decide who is suitable for what job. It is the process by which an employee comes to know of the work environment. Perception of a thing may vary from person to person. A small story will make this clear. Some blind men were asked to feel an elephant and describe it. One of them felt its foot and said, "An elephant is like a pillar." Another felt its ears and said, "It is like a waving chowrie." Another felt its trunk and said," It is like a swing." Obviously none of them could have a total perception of what an elephant would be like.

Before forming an idea about an employee, a manager should have a total perception of him. He should not be guided by one or two actions of the employee. A college principal was annoyed by the behaviour of an office staff who was coming late everyday. In spite of repeated warning, he would come late and offer some excuse or other. The principal came to know that the staff had a good voice. He encouraged him and asked him to render prayer songs in the assembly meetings. A drastic change occurred in the attitude of the employee. He started coming on time and also offered to take more responsibilities in the office work.

There are certain perceptual mechanisms by which the attitude of a person can be judged. The first one is selection. When two persons are asked to comment on a glass half filled with water, one may say that it is half empty and the other may say that it is half full. Both are true but they present different attitudes. The next one is organizing. People tend to group similar things and also resort to simplification in their activities. The third process is interpretation. An example for this is the Halo effect. People judge a person on the basis of a single trait. For example, people tend to rate a good speaker as a good leader as well.

Group Behaviour

A group is the largest set of two or more individuals who are jointly characterized by a network of relevant communications, a shared sense of collective identity and one or more shared dispositions with associated normative strength.[5]

In other words, a group is a collection of two or more people who have a common goal or interest and interact with each other to accomplish their objective; they are aware of one another and perceive themselves to be part of the group.[6]

Groups may be classified into (i) Apathetic group, (ii) Erratic group, (iii) Strategic group, and (iv) Conservative group. The apathetic group consists of low-paid members who are discontented on account of some common grievance. The erratic common group consists of semi-skilled workers who are erratic in their behaviour towards the management. The strategic group consists of skilled employees who hold

5. David Horton Smith, p. 141.

6. Rao and Narayana, p. 747.

important positions in a company. The conservative group has highly skilled workers who hesitate to plunge into common action programme.

Organizational Conflict

An organization employs persons coming from different backgrounds. Therefore, conflict between individuals and groups is inevitable in an organization. In fact, even within a single individual, there is conflict. Conflict may arise between individuals with respect to goals, values or events. Generally, we think that conflict is bad and that it disturbs normal work and so conflict must be avoided at all costs. But modern philosophers look at it from a different angle. They think that conflict is not an organizational abnormality and that it is a normal aspect of social behaviour. Instead of fighting against it, one should try to understand it. Conflict is contributive to growth and development. But for conflict, monopolistic tendencies and autocratic controls will set in and cause much more damage than the conflict itself.

Conflict is behind all changes and changes are necessary for growth. It does not mean that one should encourage conflict. One should treat conflict as a natural process and deal with it in a sensible fashion.

There are several types of conflicts which arise due to the different roles a person assumes in his life. Taking the case of a man, he is a worker in a company, a traveller in a bus, consumer in the market, husband for his wife and father for his children. As his roles increase, his conflicts also increase.

(i) *Person-role conflict:* Conflict arises when a person encounters a clash against the values he/she follows. For example, when the manager asks a clerk to prepare a fictitious account, the clerk may refuse since it is against his/her conscience to do so.

(ii) *Inter-role conflict:* When a person is asked to take up multiple roles, conflict arises. For example when a loyal worker in forced to take up the role of a union leader, he/she finds it very difficult to do justice to both.

(iii) *Inter-personal conflict:* This arises when two persons vie with each other for a post.

(iv) *Inter-group conflict:* This arises due to differences in the ideologies followed by the groups concerned.

Sanskrit Sources on Organizational Behaviour

Analysing human personality, the Upaniṣads come up with the theory that man is controlled by egos — the little ego and the pure ego. They are not two separate entities but are only two dimensions of the same ego. The pure ego is ever free and ever illumined. It is pure consciousness. It is free from pleasure and pain. It is not pain alone that affects us; pleasure can also affect us. There are instances of people who have died on hearing a happy news. But it is only the so-called pleasure attached to worldly things that can affect us, as for example, in the case of a person who is informed that he had won Rs. 10,000,000 in the lottery, he may collapse on hearing this news, being unable to contain the joy within.

But a joy that is beyond all worldly things is the real joy and the pure ego is of that form. Then there is this little ego which is tied to the body — mind complex. On account of this bondage, it experiences joys and sorrows alternately and therefore, has no peace. The *Muṇḍaka Upaniṣad* (3.1.2) says:

द्वा सुपर्णा सयुजा सखाया
समानं वृक्षं परिषस्वजाते।
तयोरन्यः पिप्पलं स्वाद्वत्ति
अनश्नन् अन्यो अभिचाकषीति।।

dvā suparṇā sayujā sakhāyā
samānaṁ vṛkṣaṁ pariṣasvajāte ।
tayoranyah pippalaṁ svādvatti
anaśnan anyo abhicākaṣīti ।।

On the self same tree, are two beautiful birds, intimate friends, with fine plumage. Among the two, one bird tastes the fruits of the tree, while the other sits in its own glory without eating the fruits.

All our troubles arise because of our mistake in identifying ourselves with the little ego. On the other hand, we can remain in perfect peace if we identify ourselves with the pure ego which is also within our hold. In other words, if an individual can succeed in freeing himself from the shackles of the body-mind nexus, he can ever remain peaceful. This is the secret behind human personality, human behaviour and the entire human psychology, for that matter. Human beings commit mistakes or even sins only because they do not realize their true nature. Swami Vivekananda would say, "Come up, O lions, and shake off the delusion that you are sheep; you are souls, immortal spirits, free, blest and eternal, ye are not matter, ye are not bodies; matter is your servant, not you the servant of matter."[7]

But does this philosophy have any relevance to management? Indeed it has; it is the duty of the managers to make their subordinates realize their potential and achieve perfection in whatever they do. The manager has to provide only the spark. It will catch up like wild fire. Just a turn of event has turned robbers into saints. It is said that Vālmīki was originally a robber. When a hunter killed its mate, the female *krauñca* bird started wailing. The scene moved Vālmīki to such an extent that he became a sage and a poet of

7. Complete Works, vol. I, p. 10.

extraordinary merit and produced the wonderful *Rāmāyaṇa*. So a quest for perfection is fundamental to all humanity. It is the true nature. The true nature can never be suppressed. It may be sometimes covered by some external substance. The prism is colourless; that is its true nature. When a red flower is placed behind it, the prism looks red. It is not its true nature. Likewise truth and straightforwardness are the true nature of man. A child cannot utter a lie. It learns what a lie is only at a later stage. Beauty is not external, but is internal. A child is attached to its mother however much ugly she may be. For the child, its mother is the most beautiful person in the world. It is charmed by the internal beauty of the love of its mother. So, truth and goodness are the real nature of every person. If there are any external factors hiding them, they should be removed. This is what every manager has to do as part of "organizational behaviour" programme. Human beings should not become slaves of an external object like money. They have the power to withstand the pressure of the sensory objects. Their sense organs are more powerful than the objects. Sense objects are gross but the sense organs are subtle. Being gross, the sense objects can be handled by us, but not the subtle sense organs. The subtle is always more powerful than the gross. The energy in the gross is inferior to that in the subtle form. The atom which is very small has so much energy within it. So are the sense organs. They have abundant energy and power. The mind is still more subtle than the sense organs. The sense organs at least have external instruments like eye, ear, etc. We know that when the eye is open, we can see things. If we do not want to see anything outside we can close the eye. But the mind is not like that. We cannot shut it out with anything. It is ever active. It is more expansive than the sense organs. The eye can see only those things that are within its range. But the mind can take us to the USA in a moment. The sense organs simply present what is before us. But the mind can assimilate, analyse, interpret (and also misinterpret) and find out truths. The eye sees that the prism is red. The mind says, "No, if it looks red it is because some red object is kept behind." We see, therefore, that mind is more powerful than the sense organs. We also see that external things do not bring peace and tranquillity to the mind. So, the Indian philosophers say, "Enough of seeing external things. Look inward, study your own mind and consciousness which alone can bring you ever-lasting peace." It is the mind that dictates terms. If the mind says, "You are bound," you feel bound. If the mind says, "you are free," you feel liberated. Hence, it is said,

मन एव मनुष्याणां कारणं बन्धमोक्षयोः।
mana eva manuṣyāṇāṁ kāraṇaṁ bandhamokṣayoḥ।

If the mind is weak, the nervous system, sensory system and in fact, every system in the body becomes weak. A man possessing a weak body but a strong mind can conquer the world. Gandhiji was a frail looking old man when he fought the British for Independence; but the entire British Empire was trembling before him. More powerful than the mind is the *buddhi* or the intellect. An example can be given. A man is attracted by the sweets tastefully stacked in a shop. The colour, the smell and the desire to taste it draw him near the sweet shop. The sense objects — the sweet, the sense organs of eye, nose and the tongue and also the mind — are all on one side. But now the *buddhi* says. "No sweet, the doctor has advised me against sweets." The *buddhi* prevails over the mind which gets controlled. If you overrule *buddhi* you get into trouble. So *buddhi* is more powerful than the mind.

Going deeper into human psychology, the *buddhi* is not actually different from the mind. It is only a state of the mind. When it is in a "doubtful" state it is called *manas* (mind). When it is in a "firm" state, it is called *buddhi.* There are two more states, namely *ahaṁkāra* and *citta.*

मनोबुद्धिरहङ्कारश्चित्तं करणमान्तरम्।
संशयो निश्चयो गर्वः स्मरणं विषया इमे।।

manobuddhirahaṅkāraścittaṁ karaṇamāntaram।
saṁśayo niścayogarvaḥ smaraṇaṁ viṣayā ime।।
— *Vedānta Paribhāṣā,* ch. I, p. 32

> The mental state is of four kinds, namely, doubt, certitude, egoism and recollection. Owing to this diversity of states, the mind, though one, is designated as *manas, buddhi, ahaṁkāra* and *citta* in the respective states.

The *buddhi,* though powerful, is not the ultimate. The one that illumines the *buddhi* is the *ātman* or the pure consciousness which is the whole and not part of anything. The body is perishable but the embodied soul is imperishable. How do we know that the soul remains inside, so as to be called as "embodied"? When we are sleeping, all the limbs are at rest. But we see a dream in which we drive a car or do this and that. When the hands and legs are at rest, what is it that drives the car? It is the subconscious mind. Sometimes, we go into a dreamless deep sleep state. At that stage, the mind is also at rest. What is active then at that stage directing our respiratory system and the like? It is the *ātman,* the pure consciousness. If it is active even when the mind is at rest, then we can imagine its power. It is subtler than the mind and hence more powerful than that. Hence, the *Gītā* says:

इन्द्रियाणि पराण्याहुः इन्द्रियेभ्यः परं मनः।
मनसस्तु परा बुद्धिः यो बुद्धेः परतस्तु सः।।

indriyāṇi parāṇyāhuḥ indriyebhyaḥ paraṁ manaḥ।
manasastu parā buddhiḥ yo buddheḥ paratastu saḥ।।
— III.42

There is a traditional story that brings out the supremacy of *ātman* over the *buddhi.* There was a sage in a forest. Somehow a cat got attached to him. But it was afraid of a dog which was roaming around near the hermitage. The cat appealed to the sage, "Please make me a dog so that I will be free from the fear of the dog." The sage transformed it into a dog by his yogic power. Once, this dog was chased by a tiger. Somehow it escaped; it again appealed to the sage, "Please make me a tiger so that I can overcome the fear." The sage made it a tiger. Then the tiger was threatened by a lion. Again at the request of the tiger, the sage transformed it into a lion which thought that it was all powerful. But it had a fear in the corner of its mind, "What will happen if the sage were to transfer me back to a dog or a cat? If I get rid of him, I can continue to be the all powerful lion." With this idea it rushed towards the sage. The sage knew its intentions and transformed it back into its original form of a cat. In a moment it lost all its power, since its *buddhi* got corrupted. The sage, the *ātmasvarūpa,* remained unaffected. We saw that the cat was afraid of one or the other at every stage. It is always the case when there is a second one co-existing. Hence, the Advaita says that there is but one and only *ātman,* undivided and unsurpassed. It exists in each and everybody but yet it is one. We call a stretch of water as Bay of Bengal, another as Arabian sea and one more as Indian ocean. But where is the difference between them? We give them name on the basis of the boundary it touches. Likewise the supreme *ātman* is just one. The bodies are only limiting adjuncts, on account of which names and forms arise. These are apparent differences which perish some time or the other but what remains unaffected is the pure consciousness. Obviously such philosophical thoughts cannot be expounded to the workers in a factory. They are more bothered about their wages, benefits and promotion. But a manager can spread the message that inequalities and imperfections are impermanent. Every worker is capable of better performance and every employee can achieve perfection in his/her work. They should be told to get rid of Y and work with a sense of detachment towards worldly things. There is a beautiful verse in Sanskrit explaining this concept:

भोगे रोगभयं कुले च्युतिभयं वित्ते नृपालाद्भयं
माने दैन्यभयं बले रिपुभयं रूपे जराया भयम्।
शास्त्रे वादिभयं गुणे खलभयं काये कृतान्ताद्भयम्
सर्वं वस्तु भयान्वितं भुवि नृणां वैराग्यमेवाभयम्।।

bhoge roga-bhayaṁ kule cyuti-bhayaṁ vitte nṛpālād-bhayaṁ
māne dainya-bhayaṁ bale ripu-bhayaṁ rūpe jarāyā-bhayaṁ ।
śāstre vādi-bhayaṁ guṇe khala-bhayaṁ kāye kṛtāntād-bhayaṁ
sarvaṁ vastu bhayānvitaṁ bhuvi nṛṇāṁ vairagyamevābahyam ।।

— *Vairāgya Śataka*, 32

Enjoyment of pleasures is accompanied by the fear of disease, noble birth has the fear of a sudden fall, wealth is exposed to danger from the rulers, dignity to misfortune, strength to fear from the enemy, beauty to danger from the old age, knowledge of scriptures to controversy, merits to danger from the wicked and the body itself to the fear of death. All things are thus beset with danger or fear. Detachment alone grants fearlessness in the world.

The need of the hour is to impress people about the value of *tapas*. *Tapas* is not just going to a forest and sitting there for hours/days. *Tapas* is concentration of the energies of the mind and the sense organs. This is what scientists do, that is, they turn their minds in scientific methods and attitudes; with that they are able to drive deep into the secrets of nature and bring out the hitherto unknown truths. Every manager and every worker has to add the value of *tapas* in their work. Without *tapas,* work becomes monotonous and a burden as well.

When *tapas* is added, work becomes interesting and enjoyable which again leads to perfection in the jobs undertaken.

The Indian philosophers prescribe two paths both of which are essential for the human society; one is *pravṛtti* and the other is *nivṛtti*. The first one is an action-oriented path and the latter is an inward process marked by deep thinking, meditation, spiritual knowledge, renunciation, service and sacrifice. The first one, namely, *pravṛtti mārga,* is useful to us as far as we are concerned with materialism and consumerism. But there will be a stage when these things will be of no use. There is a story. There was a learned man in a town on the bank of a river. One day he wanted to go to a city on the other bank for giving a lecture. He came to the river bank and engaged a boatman for crossing the river. On the way, he engaged the boatman in a conversation in order to pass time. He asked the boatman. "Do you know *vyākaraṇa* (grammar)?" The boatman said "No." The scholar told him, "You have wasted 25 per cent of your life." He asked him again, "Do you know logic?" The boatman answered him in the negative. The scholar told him that he had wasted another 25 per cent of his life. The learned man asked once again, "Do you know astrology?" Again the boatman said "no"; the scholar told him, "Without knowing these, you have wasted 75 per cent of your life." Before he could ask the next question, the boatman asked the scholar, "Sir, do you know swimming?" The scholar said, "No." Now the boatman said, "Sir, you have wasted 100 per cent of your life; the boat has developed a crack and water is rushing into the boat. In a few minutes, it will sink." So saying, the boatman jumped into the river, swam across and saved his life. The scholar, unfortunate that he was, entered a watery grave. Money, power, position and property have relevance only up to a certain level. Beyond that they will create problems. The *nivṛtti mārga* and self-introspection are necessary at this stage. One has to think of human values, morals and ethics. Both *pravṛtti mārga* and *nivṛtti mārga* can co-exist together in every walk of life. A manager has to keep in mind that he/she cannot always get things done by the rule of law. He/She has to appeal to the human values directly or indirectly, with respect to the members of his/her team. He/She has to concentrate on co-operative endeavour and team spirit. He/She has to set an example for others by entertaining positive attitudes, habits and mould his/her ways on the basis of environmental conditions. Instead of asking team members to do what he/she likes, he/she should create opportunities to bring out their creativity.

The subordinates should not be considered as slaves. They should be engaged in meaningful discussion on development activities. Good ideas can emanate from them also. A good manager should follow the grand idea of the Vedic seers.

आ नो भद्राः क्रतवो यन्तु विश्वतः।
ā no bhadrāḥ kratavo yantu viśvataḥ
— *Ṛgveda*

Let noble thoughts come to us from all directions.

A similar idea is set forth in the *Manu-Smṛti*.

श्रद्दधानः शुभां विद्यां आददीत् अवरादपि।
अन्त्यादपि परं धर्मं स्त्रीरत्नं दुष्कुलादपि।।

śraddhadānaḥ śubhāṁ vidyāṁ ādadīt avarādapi।
antyādapi paraṁ dharmaṁ strītanaṁ duṣkulādapi।।
— 12.6071

> Seek good knowledge with great attention, even from the lowly placed. Learn virtue even from the downtrodden. Take a gem of a woman as wife even from the backward community.

The workers should be told to fight against evils and imperfections themselves. The virtuous should not be weak and submissive. The very basis of virtue is strength, love, compassion and non-violence all of which are based on mental strength. Mental strength is the only answer to tensions, depression and fear. A mind affected by fear and grief loses the power of discrimination. A manager has to be calm and steady, but at same time bold and firm. Fear can be driven away by faith and self-belief. Fearlessness does not mean being impetuous and indiscriminate. Fearlessness should be backed by calmness and compassion. Some weak-minded people take to alcohol to overcome their tension. It must be borne in mind that one weakness cannot remove another weakness. Dirt cannot remove dirt. One must wash away dirt through pure water. Likewise weakness or fear can be removed only by strength. One cannot escape from problems by taking to alcohol or any such intoxicating substance. A manager has to do sound counselling to such weak members of his/her team and make them mentally strong.

The *Bhagavad-Gītā* says:

यस्मान्नोद्विजते लोको लोकान्नोद्विजते च यः।
yasmānnodvijate loko lokānnodvijate ca yaḥ।
— 12.15

"He is a man who does not frighten the world and he, in turn, is not frightened by the world." Such a person has no enemies in the world. In the *Mahābhārata*, Dharmaputra is called *ajātaśatru*, "one for whom no enemies are born." We may have a doubt here. Is not Duryodhana an enemy of Dharmaputra;

so how can we call him "enemy-less"? The epithet does not mean that there were no enemies for Dharmaputra. But Dharmaputra did not consider any body as his enemy. There is a *subhāṣita*.

> उपकारिषु यः साधुः साधुत्वे तस्य को गुणः
> अपकारिषु यः साधुः स साधुः सद्भिरुच्यते॥
>
> *upakāriṣu yaḥ sādhuḥ sādhutve tasya ko guṇaḥ*
> *apakāriṣu yaḥ sādhuḥ sa sādhuḥ sadbhiḥ ucyate*
> — *Pañcatantra*, I.270

> Where is the merit in a person who is good only to those who have helped him? He is a noble man who is good, even to those who have harmed him.

The Indian philosophy has another beautiful idea for the managers. It says, "Build up your character; your life is your own work, your own privilege. Do not leave it to others. Take help form anybody, but the work is your own. And when you develop, the world will marvel; here is one who with given capital of psychic energy, has built-up a huge business of intellectual and spiritual life, just like any businessman starting with a thousand rupees capital, later on becomes a millionaire, because he invested it properly and worked hard. The same thing holds good in the case of human personality."[8]

A manager might have studied all aspects of business organization quite well. But unless he/she is going to apply what he/she has studied, his/her study is of no use. Books are only pointers. A good manager should be able to learn from his/her practical experience, analyse the attitudes of each and every employee working under him/her and put them in their proper shape. Sri Ramakrishna gives an illustration in

8. Swami Ranganathananda, vol. I.

this context. The almanac forecasts that so many inches of rain will fall this year. But if you take the almanac and squeeze it, you will not get a drop of water out of it. Similarly, the theoretical knowledge of the attitudes will not help a manager much. He/She has to study each and every individual under his/her care and chalk out his/her own plans to mould them into a unit of force.

A manager must think of contributing something original for the growth of the people around him/her. Even if he/she transforms one single individual and guides him/her into proper work culture, it is a worthwhile effort, rather than ambling along with mediocre performance. The *Mahābhārata* says:

मुहूर्तं ज्वलतो श्रेयो न तु धूमयितुं चिरम्।
muhūrtaṁ jvalato śreyo na tu dhūmayituṁ ciram।

It is better you flame forth for one instant than smoke away for ages.

How should the personality be built? It should be built on a sound rock of pure inner consciousness so that no external force can shake it. Money, power and positions are quicksands. If the personality is built on them, it will fall no sooner than it is built. The best way to root out corruption from the country is to help people mould their personality on the firm ground of spirituality. Spirituality, in Swami Vivekananda's words, is nothing but faith in oneself and a concern for fellow human beings. Love and compassion can bring about wholesale changes in the attitudes of people. A manager with love and compassion will have nothing to fear. He/She will always be cheerful. Ādi Śaṅkarācārya says in his *Vivekacūḍāmaṇi* (343):

निर्धनोऽपि सदा तुष्टोऽप्यसहायो महाबलः।
नित्यतृप्तोऽप्यभुंजानोऽप्यसमः समदर्शनः।।

nirdhano 'pi sadā tuṣṭo 'pyasāhāyo mahābalaḥ ।
nityatṛpto 'pyabhuṁjāno 'pyasamaḥ samadarśanaḥ ॥

That person is an extraordinary person who though has no wealth, no power, no resources, is yet full of joy, full of cheer; though he has no helpers, is infinitely strong; ever satisfied though not experiencing sense pleasures; though he is incomparable he looks upon all others as his equal.

All problems arise only when we consider ourselves superior to others. The superiority complex overshadows our outlook. Compassion and love take the backseat; authoritarian tendency and arrogance come to the forefront. Consequently, others get offended and begin to hate him/her. If the manager desists from such an attitude, he/she can handle any situation in a better fashion. In Japan, the MD of a company will also be working along with ordinary workers, wearing a similar uniform. Workers' participation in administration is followed as a policy in major companies in Japan.

In Kālidāsa's *Kumārasambhavam* (V.77), we have a beautiful scene. When there are allegations against Lord Śiva, Pārvatī defends him stoutly. The main allegation is that Śiva indulges in inauspicious practices like dancing in the cemetery to which Pārvatī replies.

अकिञ्चनः सन् प्रभवः स सम्पदां त्रिलोकनाथः पितृसद्मगोचरः।
स भीमरूपः शिव इत्युदीर्यते न सन्ति याथार्थ्यविदः पिनाकिनः॥

akiñcanaḥ san prabhavaḥ sa sampadāṁ trilokanāthaḥ pitṛsadmagocaraḥ ।
sa bhīmarūpaḥ śiva ityudīryate na santi yāthārthyavidaḥ pinākinaḥ ॥

He, who has nothing for himself, is the source of all riches; being the Lord of the three worlds, yet he is the occupant of

> the cemetery; being terrible in appearance, still he is called "Śiva," the auspicious. There is none who has known him truly.

Lord Śiva's form reflects the true spirit of Indian philosophy, that is, renunciation. There is no merit in speaking of renunciation when you do not have a thing. Renunciation is, being detached from something when you have it. This is how a manager should function. He/She has position and power but they actually do not belong to him/her. If he/she goes about proclaiming, "I am the manager, I am the manager," nobody will respect him/her. Power has glory only when it is kept in check; when it is expended, it loses its merit. In days of yore, there were sages who could curse anybody by the power of their penance. But if they did so, they lost the power of their penance as well. Value of human life is greater than that of money and power. Though in command of everything, yet the manager should function as though they do not belong to him. Otherwise complexes develop and the gap between him/her and his/her team members goes on widening. Co-ordination and team spirit will definitely suffer. One has to give up external attractions in a natural way, in order to realize something greater within oneself.

One of the problems that mars interpersonal relationship in an organizational set-up is anger. In an angry mood, we utter some nonsense and do some action hurriedly. Though we may realize after sometime that what we did was wrong, ego prevents us from making amends by saying a simple word, "sorry" to the party concerned. So, suppressing our conscience, we try to justify our action or utter a lie by saying, "I did not say so." The whole thing spoils our character. At the very first instance, the anger should have been controlled. It is very difficult to control anger, but we have to train the mind in controlling anger. By repeated exercise of will power and dedication to higher causes, we can slowly overcome the low emotions of fear, hatred, pride and anger. No emotion, including anger, is bad by itself, according to psychology. But one must know how to handle them. Anger has a place in human life. When we see some injustice going on around us, we must rouse our indignation, but in a controlled way.

Unless you have anger, you cannot react properly to it. We have a relevant incident in Kālidāsa's *Śākuntalam*. On account of Durvāsā's curse, Duṣyanta fails to recognize Śakuntalā whom he had married secretly in the forest. Unable to bear the insult, Śakuntalā appeals to her mother Menakā who takes her away to the heavenly region. Meanwhile the ring (a token of recognition that had been given by the king during their secret meeting) which Śakuntalā had lost in a tank on her journey is brought by a fisherman. On seeing the ring, the king recollects the entire episode and starts lamenting for his action. Day after day his grief mounts.

Now comes a news that his friend, the *vidūṣaka* has been seized by some evil spirit and confined to a lonely place. The king's anger is aroused and he immediately takes up his bow and releases his friend. It was Indra's idea to arouse his anger and infuse the heroic spirit once again in him since he wanted the king's services in a battle against the demons.

All our people must be educated on how to channellize their anger for socially useful purpose. Righteous indignation is as much necessary as control of anger. We do not show anger where it ought to be shown, but direct it on helpless dependants at home. On the other hand, we must take the energy of anger and use it for some good purpose. That is how we can build up good character and develop a good personality.[9]

Managers dislike people who take leave or go on an LTC tour. The Manager feels that the employee is shirking work

---

9. Swami Ranganathananda, vol. I.

while the employee feels that the manager is trying to prevent him/her from taking the eligible leave. The extremes of both the cases are undesirable. There are also certain work alcoholics. They would not spend even ten minutes a day with their family. In families where both the parents are busy throughout the day all through the year, the children long for parental love and when it is not forthcoming they turn out to be vagabonds and criminals. He/She is a wise person who is able to apportion his/her time equitably between work and leisure. One who does not know how to utilize his/her leisure properly will not be able to concentrate on his/her work either. One should know what is action, what is inaction and what is forbidden action. The *Gītā* says.

कर्मणो ह्यपि बोद्धव्यं बोद्धव्यं च विकर्मणः।
अकर्मणश्च बोद्धव्यं गहना कर्मणो गतिः।।

karmaṇo hyapi boddhavyaṁ boddhavyaṁ ca vikarmaṇaḥ।
akarmaṇaśca boddhavyaṁ gahanā karmaṇo gatiḥ।।

— 4.17

For verily (the true nature) even of action should be known, as also, forbidden action and inaction; the nature of *karma* is deep and impenetrable.

Swami Ranganathananda[10] quotes from L.P. Jacks (*Education of the Whole man*): Labour turns into leisure when art is applied to it. Leisure turns into labour when science traces it to its roots. Today, to have leisure is to be at the mercy of other people. A man is no longer the maker of his leisure. Today, the more leisure a man has, the more active he is in destroying others' leisure and they his leisure. Leisure is the time we spend in mutual botheration. When labour merely tires the body without involving the mind, even leisure becomes

10. Ibid., vol. I, p. 429.

irksome. Man utilizes leisure largely in search of external excitements. That brings in unwanted problems. How then to use leisure? The *Gītā* gives the solution.

कर्मण्यकर्मः यः पश्येत् अकर्मणि च कर्म यः।
स बुद्धिमान् मनुष्येषु स युक्तः कृत्स्नकर्मकृत्।।

karmaṇyakarmaḥ yaḥ paśyet akarmaṇi ca karma yaḥ ।
sa buddhimān manuṣyeṣu sa yuktaḥ kṛtsnakarmakṛt ।।
— 4.18

One who sees inaction in action, and action in inaction, is intelligent among human beings. He is a *yogī* and a doer of all action.

"No work" is real work and work is no work at all. In other words, work should be done as though it is leisure, so that it becomes enjoyable. If work is attended to with struggle and tension, then it becomes a burden. When it is a burden, the tendency is to escape from it. That is why majority of the people dislike work and therefore shirk away from it. Managers should teach their team members to love work and enjoy doing it. For doing that, the managers must enjoy their work themselves, first.

There is a beautiful stanza from the *Aṣṭāvakra Gītā* (18.61):

निवृत्तिरपि मूढस्य प्रवृत्तिरूपजायते।
प्रवृत्तिरपि धीरस्य निवृत्ति फल भागिनि।।

nivṛttirapi mūḍhasya pravṛtti-rūpajāyate ।
pravṛttirapi dhīrasya nivṛtti phala bhāgini ।।

Inactivity of a foolish man transforms itself into activity; the activity of a wise man, contributes to the fruits of inactivity or inaction.

There are some people who will be thinking about their office even when they are on a holiday. It does no good either for them or for their office. A wise man would enjoy his work as though it is leisure.

Many organizational problems arise since we do not understand human nature. According to Indian philosophers, the human nature is based on three *guṇa*s (or forces) namely *sattva, rajas* and *tamas. Sattva* is calmness and serenity. *Rajas* is energy and enthusiasm. *Tamas* is inertia and laziness. Every human being, for that matter, the whole nature, is made up of these three qualities. They may be present in varying degrees in each one of us. That is why some people are more energetic or lazier than others. In one and the same person, one or the other quality may dominate at different times. If *rajas* dominates we behave rudely; if *sattva* is more powerful, we behave calmly. The advice of the *Gītā* is that we should not be enslaved by the *guṇa*s. "Go beyond them," says the *Gītā*.

गुणान्येतान्–अतीत्य त्रीन् देही देहसमुद्भवान्।
जन्ममृत्युजरादुःखैः विमुक्तः अमृतमश्नुते।।

guṇān etan atītya trīṇ dehi dehasamudbhavān ।
janma mṛtyu jarā duḥkhaiḥ vimuktaḥ amṛtaṁ aśnute ।।

— 14.20

Having transcended the three *guṇa*s which have produced the body, and freed from birth, death, old age and sorrow, he enjoys immortality.

What is meant by "going beyond the *guṇa*s?" An illustration will make it clear. When somebody abuses you, the first reaction is to retaliate, abuse him/her back in more severe terms. In other words, we allow the *rajo-guṇa* to dominate. If, on the other hand, you simply ignore his/her abuse, he/she will go away after some time. Disintegrate his/her sentences into words. For example, if he/she had said "you are a fool," the first three words are not abusive. Only the last word "fool" is offending. (A well-experienced man said, "If somebody calls you a fool, don't open your mouth and prove it!") Disintegrate the word "fool" into letters. Does the letter "f" or "o" "l" offend you? They are after all sounds. This kind of analysis will bring in peace. Most of the problems could be solved if people are taught to make this kind of an analysis. By such a process, one develops inner strength by which many great things could be achieved. The *Gītā* further says:

मानापमानयोः तुल्यः तुल्यो मित्रारिपक्षयोः।
सर्वारम्भपरित्यागी गुणातीतः स उच्यते॥

mānāpamānayoḥ tulyaḥ tulyo mitrāripakṣayoḥ।
sarvārambha parityāgī guṇātītaḥ sa ucyate॥
— 14.25

He who treats honour and disgrace on equal footing, is equally disposed towards friend and foe, and has renounced the sense of doership in all undertakings — he is said to have risen above the three *guṇa*s.

In the Chapter XVI of the *Gītā*, a series of noble qualities are listed. One or two verses may be quoted here.

अभयं सत्त्वसंशुद्धिः ज्ञानयोगव्यवस्थितिः
दानं दमश्च यज्ञश्च स्वाध्यायस्तपआर्जवम्॥

abhayaṁ sattva saṁśuddhiḥ jñāna yoga vyavasthitiḥ।
dānaṁ damaśca yajñaś ca svādhyāyas tapa ārjavam॥
— 16.1

Fearlessness, purity of heart, steadfastness in knowledge, alms giving, control of senses, sacrifice, study of scriptures, austerity, uprightness.

One of the qualities mentioned in the succeeding verse is *mārdava* or gentleness. One can be gentle yet firm. One should not allow the "gentleness" to be misconstrued as weakness. Gentleness has its own power. There was a wrestling champion. He conquered everybody by the strength of his might. But before his wife, he was quiet like a pet dog. The wife conquered him by her gentleness of love. A *Mahābhārata* verse says (III.29.30):

मृदुना मार्दवं हन्ति मृदुना हान्ति दारुणम्।
नासाध्यं मृदुना किञ्चत् तस्मात् तीक्ष्णतरो मृदुः।।

mṛdunā mārdavaṁ hanti mṛdunā hanti dāruṇam।
na asādhyaṁ mṛdunā kiñcit tasmāt tīkṣṇataro mṛduḥ।।

> The gentle conquers the gentle. The gentle conquers the hard. There is nothing that gentleness cannot conquer. Therefore gentleness is the highest virtue. Gentleness is the most powerful thing, the most penetrating thing.

Swami Ranganathananda explains it with an example. A drop of water falls on a piece of rock everyday, every moment. The rock is cut in course of time by the impact of the gentle water drop.

Certain cultural factors, even food habits, contribute to the nature of a person. According to the *Gītā* (XVII, vv. 8 to 10), sweet and bland foods are dear to serene people. Bitter, acidic, salted, pungent and spicy food is liked by the energetic people, while the people dominated by inertia like food which is half cooked, insipid and putrid.

The *Gītā* advocates *tapas*, that is, austerity in all our endeavours. Work is to be done for the sake of work, with a view to excel in them, without aspiring for personal benefits out of the work done. If work is done for deriving benefits or for the sake of ostentation, it becomes *rājasika*. If there is no element of sacrifice in the work done, it becomes *tāmasika*. Austerity is recommended in every field of activity physical, mental or speech.

A study of the *Bhagavad-Gītā* will be really helpful for a manager in every sphere of his activity, especially in the analysis of organizational behaviour.

10

Social Responsibility

Need for Social Responsibility

The Industrial Revolution that took place in England in the nineteenth century brought with it some evils as well. The mill owners wanted quick profit in double quick time. They squeezed the workers and extracted more and more work from them. No attention was paid to working conditions. Consequently, labour problems arose and the state had to intervene. Several legislations were passed in the parliaments all over the world, protecting the rights and privileges of the working class. Industries flourished, production increased, goods were marketed and consumed. As the size and production level of the goods increased, waste products also increased. Industries required a large amount of water and so they were located on the banks of rivers. It was easy for the industries to dispose of the waste as well. Effluents were simply led into the rivers and washed away. The damage was hardly noticeable in the beginning but within a few years, it grew to enormous proportions.

Some of the chemical industries release poisonous gases and toxic substances that are injurious to the environment and health of the people living in the vicinities of the company. It is generally believed that an industrial establishment provides job opportunities to a large number of people and therefore the society should be obliged to them. But a different kind of thinking has developed in recent times. The contemporary thinking is that organizations operate only because society grants them the right to do so and this right will continue only so long as society is satisfied with its results.[1] The stakeholders of a company are many: creditors, debtors, suppliers, employees, customers, dealers, consumers and the general public at large. A company owes social responsibility to all of them. Modern managers have to cope with the problem of social responsibility and it is indeed a big challenge for them. They have to deal with the demands of employees, provide maximum dividends to shareholders, comply with governmental rules, maintain the quality of products, achieve customer satisfaction and follow business ethics while dealing with competitors. They also have to take care of pollution control, effluent treatment, support to education and upliftment of the downtrodden.

Definition of Social Responsibility

Social responsibility may be defined as a firm's obligation to constituent groups in society, beyond that prescribed by law or union contract.[2] A few important aspects of social responsibility are highlighted in this definition. An organization is obliged not only to its employees but also to the society whose resources like land, air and water are made use of by the firm. It is not enough if the company abides by the statutory laws and provides basic amenities for its workers. Social responsibility demands that they must go beyond the law, bear some more responsibility of their own accord and cater to the needs of the society at large.

---

1. Parker, Robert and Henry Ellbert, p. 5.
2. T.M. Jones, *Management Review*, pp. 59-60.

Why Social Responsibility?

While social responsibility is an important concept, it cannot be thrust on the companies. No one can force them to take it up and there is no legal binding on the companies to take up social responsibility. But it is a moral responsibility and the society expects them to help its cause. Having taken the resources of the society, it is the duty of a company to use its resources to help the society. Acts of societal responsibility will be a source of advertisement for the company and its profits are likely to increase in the long run. If the business does not help the society's needs, the society will press for more benefits from its government which in turn, will have to pressurize companies to pay more tax. The responsibility taken up by the organizations will reduce the burden of the governments which can concentrate more on other developmental activities. Social responsibility is bound to boost the image of the company. Instead of looking at companies with suspicion (that they are making a lot of money at our cost), people will look at them with respect. By voluntarily taking up social responsibility, firms can avoid government regulations regarding them. It is true that the programmes on social responsibility involves costs and it will only increase the overheads but it will bring back dividends in the form of goodwill which is an indirect profit to a company.

Total Responsibility

Community development programme is not the only responsibility of the industry. They have responsibility towards all the stakeholders of the company. Their responsibility must be taken in totality so that their attention could be equitably divided among all the stakeholders. In fact, even social responsibility can be better understood in the light of the total responsibility that they have.

RESPONSIBILITY TO THE OWNERS

The owners of the company have invested a lot of money while establishing the company and they would have also ploughed back their profit into the company. The company is committed to the proper utilization of funds invested by the owners. It should also be ensured that they get a fair rate of return for their investments. The company executives are also expected to keep the owners informed of the business operations that are taking place from time to time.

RESPONSIBILITY TO THE EMPLOYEES

The employees must get their due wages on time. They must be provided with basic and good working conditions and amenities. Facilities must be provided for their training and development. They must be provided with proper environment to improve their efficiency. Health care, housing, provident fund and such other facilities must be provided.

RESPONSIBILITY TO SHAREHOLDERS

Shareholders have invested their money in the hope of getting good returns. It is the responsibility of the company that the shareholders' interests are taken care of.

RESPONSIBILITY TO CUSTOMERS

The customers are the backbone of the company. They must be assured of quality goods at reasonable prices. The gullibility of the people should not be exploited by over-exaggerated statements in advertisements and high-pressure publicity.

RESPONSIBILITY TO CREDITORS AND SUPPLIERS

The creditors have agreed to supply goods only on the good faith that the company is sound and that their dues will be cleared within a reasonable time. It is, therefore, the responsibility of the company to keep them informed about their financial stability. The bills due for the creditors must be cleared within a reasonable time so that they continue to have confidence in the company. The creditors must be treated as equal partners in the progress of the company.

RESPONSIBILITY TO GOVERNMENT

Every company is expected to follow the government norms that are prescribed from time to time. The company should not get involved in any illegal operation like hoarding, black marketing, etc. Taxes and charges should be paid on time. A company should avoid bribing the government officials to get things done quickly. In import or export operations, the laws existing in the land of operation (foreign countries) must be respected and honoured.

RESPONSIBILITY TO COMPETITORS

Competition is an aid to progress. If there are no competitors, stagnation will set in and there will be no growth. A company should treat the competitors honourably and should not cause inconvenience to them either covertly or overtly. Competition is good but cut-throat competition is bad. Undue comparison and mischievous advertisements bringing down the reputation of the competitor must be avoided. Aiming to ruin a competitor, some companies reduce the price of commodities drastically, by reducing the quality. Such unethical practices should be avoided.

RESPONSIBILITY TO SOCIETY

India is still plagued by two evils, namely, poverty and illiteracy. Every company, nay every individual, in this country should help the government in eradicating these two ills of the society. Education is the panacea for all evils, said Swami Vivekananda. Companies may establish schools and colleges in order to spread education among masses. Companies also have the responsibility of preserving the environment, ecological balance and reduce pollution. They have to provide employment opportunities to the people of the area. They may conduct community meetings to bring about communal harmony. Efforts may be taken to spread message among masses on AIDS awareness, drug abuse, and other social causes. Companies may also contribute towards urban rehabilitation, development of small entrepreneurs and general awareness of hygiene.

Business Ethics

Ethics are certain standard principles or code of conduct that govern the actions and behaviour of individuals within a particular social group or an organization. They provide the basics for determining what is right or wrong in terms of a given situation. Ethics are important for business since it involves a lot of people coming from different strata of the society. A common code of conduct is necessary to control the behaviour of the employees. Some are written in the contract while some exist as unwritten rules.

The behaviour of an individual is controlled by various factors. His/Her behaviour remains more or less the same throughout his/her life, though there could be some exceptional cases where a certain incident in his/her life changes a person's entire behaviour and personality. A person who exhibits good behaviour at home cannot be totally different in the workplace or vice versa. But the liberties one takes at home cannot be taken in the workplace. A common code of conduct is necessary in a workplace. The behaviour of an individual employee and the group is linked to the image of a company as a whole and therefore certain basic ethics are considered essential in every business establishment. Ethical principles followed as a policy in a company also reflect on the conduct of its employees. For example, if a company evades taxes, the employees will indulge in pilfering and stealing the company's material.

Ethical principles change from company to company. They cannot be the same for all companies. For example, truth and transparency are expected of all the organizations. But, this may not be applicable to a company selling used cars. The buyer knows that if it is in a good condition the original owner would not have sold the car at all. Even here, a seller must be truthful by saying, "These are the defects which I have rectified. It will have a trouble free run for two years for which I will give the guarantee." He will have a better business than a person who hides the defects and makes a sale.

The factors that influence an organization to follow business ethics are: government legislation, company laws, social pressures and internal checks. Some of the avoidable unethical practices are: suppression of the profits to evade taxes, giving bribes, using company property for personal use, breaking contracts, ruining the fortunes of competitors and deceiving the public through exaggerated claims through advertisements. If the companies themselves do not come forward to stop such practices, they will be forced to do so by governments or the court of law.

Social Responsibility from Sanskrit Sources

Sanskrit literature speaks of social responsibility in the context of *paropakāra*. At the outset, the term may mean "helping others." But the Sanskrit sources emphasize *paropakāra* as an obligation and as the responsibility of groups and individuals. The entire system of values is imparted through the concepts of *puṇya* (merit) and *pāpa* (sin). A *subhāṣita* defines these two terms in a succinct manner.

श्लोकार्धेन प्रवक्ष्यामि यदुक्तं ग्रन्थकोटिषु।
परोपकारः पुण्याय पापाय परपीडनम्।।

ślokārdhena pravakṣyāmi yaduktaṁ granthakoṭiṣu ।
paropakāraḥ puṇyāya pāpāya parapīḍanam ।।

I shall state in half a stanza what has been told by crores of scriptures. Helping others leads to merit and harming others results in sin.

All values that were called as *puṇya karma* must be treated as social obligation or social responsibility in the present-day context.

Another verse says that *paropakāra* must be done by offering money or even by offering one's own life. The merit acquired by *paropakāra* cannot be equalled by hundreds of sacrifices.

परोपकारः कर्तव्यः प्राणैरपि धनैरपि।
परोपकारजं पुण्यं न स्यात् क्रतुशतैरपि।।

paropakāraḥ kartavyaḥ prāṇairapi dhanairapi ।
paropakārajaṁ puṇyaṁ na syāt kratuśatairapi ।।

— *Su*, v.1, p. 74

"Money and life are impermanent. It is better to sacrifice them for the sake of others," says another stanza.

धनानि जीवितं चैव परार्थे प्राज्ञ उत्सृजेत्।
तन्निमित्तं वरं त्यागो विनाशे नियते सति।।

dhanāni jīvitaṁ caiva parārthe prājña utsṛjet ।
tannimittaṁ varaṁ tyāgo vināśe niyate sati ।।

— Ibid., v.2

All knowledge can be drawn from nature. The concept of *paropakāra* has also been demonstrated by nature.

रविचन्द्रौघना वृक्षा नदी गावश्च सज्जनाः।
एते परोपकाराय युगे देवेन निर्मिताः।।

ravicandrau ghanā vṛkṣā nadī gāvaśca sajjanāḥ।
ete paropakārāya yuge devena nirmitāḥ॥
— Ibid., v.3

The sun, moon, clouds, trees, river, cows and noble men are created by god for (demonstrating) *paropakāra*.

Explaining how these become symbols of *paropakāra*, another verse says:

पद्माकरं दिनकरो विकचं करोति
चन्द्रो विकासयति कैरवचक्रवालम्।
नाभ्यर्थितो जलधरोऽपि जलं ददाति
सन्तः स्वयं परहितेषु कृताभियोगाः॥

padmākaraṁ dinakaro vikacaṁ karoti
candro vikāsayati kairava cakravālam।
nābhyarthito jaladharo 'pi jalaṁ dadāti
santaḥ svayaṁ parahiteṣu kṛtābhiyogāḥ॥
— Ibid., v.13

The sun causes the lotuses to bloom and the moon, the clusters of lilies. Without being prayed for, the clouds shower waters (rains): Noble men are spontaneously well disposed towards the welfare of others.

A beautiful idea is set forth in another stanza:

श्रोत्रं श्रुतेनैव न कुण्डलेन दानेन पाणिर्नतु कङ्कणेन।
विभाति कायः खलु सज्जनानां परोपकारेण न चन्दनेन॥

śrotram śrutenaiva na kuṇḍalena dānena pāṇirna tu kaṅkaṇena।
vibhāti kāyaḥ khalu sajjanānāṁ paropakāreṇa na candanena॥
— Ibid., v.12

> The ear shines only by learning and not by earrings, the hand, by giving alms and not by bracelet; the body of noble men shines by helping others but not by applying sandal paste.

As part of their social responsibility, companies may help the community by establishing schools and colleges. Providing education is the best form of service. The importance of education is extolled often in literature, as in,

> न चोरहार्यं न च राजहार्यं
> न भ्रातृभाज्यं न च भारकारि।
> व्यये कृते वर्धत एव नित्यं
> विद्याधनं सर्वधनप्रधानम्।।
>
> *na corahāryaṁ na ca rājahāryaṁ*
> *na bhrātṛ bhājyaṁ na ca bhārakāri*।
> *vyaye kṛte vardhata eva nityaṁ*
> *vidyādhanaṁ sarvadhanapradhānam*।।
>
> — Ibid., v.13, p. 30
>
> The wealth of education is the best of wealth since it cannot be stolen by thieves; it cannot be carried away by kings; it cannot be divided among brothers as a matter of right; it is never a source of burden; when it is spent it grows all the more.

Charity is another virtue that is praised often.

> गौरवं प्राप्यते दानान्नतु वित्तस्य सञ्चयात्।
> स्थितिरुच्चैः पयोदानां पयोधीनामधः स्थितिः।।
>
> *gauravaṁ prāpyate dānannatu vittasya sañcayāt*।
> *sthitiruccaiḥ payodānāṁ payodhīnāmadhaḥ sthitiḥ*।।
>
> — Ibid., v.7, p. 69
>
> A man attains dignity only by giving away his wealth to others and not by accumulating it for himself. The clouds

(which shower waters for the sake of others) have a high position (in the sky) whereas the sea (which has accumulated water) has a low position.

What companies and industries are expected to do as part of their social responsibility is service to the society, which is recommended in Sanskrit sources as well.

One particular verse says,

दानाय लक्ष्मीः सुकृताय विद्या
चिन्ता परब्रह्मविनिश्चयाय।
परोपकाराय वचांसि यस्य
वन्द्यस्त्रिलोकितिलकः स एव॥

dānāya lakṣmīḥ sukṛtāya vidyā
cintā parabrahma-viniścayāya ।
paropakārāya vacāṁsi yasya
vandyāstrilokitilakaḥ sa eva ॥
— Ibid., v.179, p.49, also *Śārṅgadharapaddhati*, v.463

Wealth should be spent for others, education for righteous deeds, words for helping others and thoughts for ultimate emancipation.

By taking upon itself the task of social responsibility a company has to alleviate the fears of the public (fears such as over exploiting the resources and causing pollution); it has to render them *abhaya* (absence of fear).

न गोप्रदानं न महीप्रदानं
न चान्नदानं हि तथा प्रधानम्।
यथा वदन्तीह बुधः प्रधानं
सर्व प्रदानेष्वभयप्रदानम्॥

na gopradānaṁ na mahīpradānaṁ
na cānnadānaṁ hi tathā pradhānaṁ ।

yathā vadantīha budhaḥ pradhānaṁ
sarva pradāneṣvabhayapradānam ||
— See Gopala Iyengar, v.86

Charity in terms of cows, land and food are not important. Wise men say that the offer of *abhaya* (freedom from fear) is the best among charitable acts.

Illustration is drawn from nature (the trees) with respect to social welfare.

छायामन्यस्य कुर्वन्ति स्वयं तिष्ठन्ति चातपे।
फलानि च परार्थेषु नात्महेतोर्महाद्रुमा:।।

chāyāmanyasya kurvanti svayaṁ tiṣṭhanti cātape |
phalanti ca parārtheṣu nātmahetormahā drumāḥ ||
— *Su*, v.4, p. 236

The *Vidura-Nīti* gives a number of clues to social responsibility. What is given for kings in the text should be taken as equivalent to company executives in the present-day context. A king should not think that whatever he has is his own. It belongs to the society.

नाममात्रेण तुष्येत छत्रेण च महीपति:।
भृत्येभ्यो विसृजेत् अर्थान् नैक: सर्वहरो भवेत्।।

nāmamātreṇa tuṣyeta chatreṇa ca mahī-patiḥ |
bhṛtyebhyo visṛjet arthān na ekaḥ sarvaharo bhavet ||
— VI.26

A king should be satisfied with his own name and the sign of legal power. He should distribute wealth among those who serve him. He should never take everything for himself.

The companies should function in a similar manner. Part of what they have earned must be spent for the welfare of the society.

While helping the society, the executives should not give room for any pride in their heart. They should have humility in their approach and they should think that they had got an opportunity to serve the society. The *Vidura-Nīti* says (VI.35):

अविसंवादनं दानं समयस्य-अव्यतिक्रमः।
आवर्तयन्ति भूतानि सम्यक् प्रणिहिता च वाक्॥

avisaṁvādanaṁ dānaṁ samayasya avyatikramaḥ।
āvartayanti bhūtāni samyak praṇihitā ca vāk॥
— VI.35

Charity for the sake of charity, not exceeding the time limit (for keeping promises) and well-equipped words win over all people.

Both the society and the industry should derive benefit from each other. They are mutually dependent and exist with mutual support. The *Vidura-Nīti* says:

अन्योन्य समुपष्टं भादन्योन्योपाश्रयेण च।
ज्ञातयः सम्प्रवर्धन्ते सरसीवोत्पलान्युत॥

anyonya samupaṣṭambhādanyonyopāśrayeṇa ca।
jñatayaḥ saṁpravardhante sarasīvotpalānyuta॥
— IV.65

With mutual support and with mutual dependence, relatives prosper verily like the water lilies in the lake.

The water lilies are nourished by the water in the lake and the latter is beautified by the presence of the former. Likewise the companies and society can prosper by mutual support.

A company may have money power, government support and a strong security. The people in the area may be scattered and powerless. But yet the company is bound by the obligation of social responsibility. It should not suppress them and cause injustice. The *Vidura-Nīti* says:

> न तद्बलं यन्मृदुना विरुध्यते सूक्ष्मो धर्मस्तरसा सेवितव्यः।
> प्रध्वंसिनी क्रूरसमाहिता श्री–मृदुप्रौढा गच्छति पुत्रपौत्रान्॥
> *na tadbalaṁ yan mr̥dunā virudhyate sūkṣmo dharmas tarasā sevitavyaḥ*।
> *pradhvaṁsinī krūrasamāhitā śrīr mr̥dupraudhā gacchati putrapautrān*॥
> — IV.71

It is not strength which is pitted against softness. Subtle justice is to be pursued after, by strength. Prosperity won by cruel means is doomed to perish, while that acquired by gentle and dignified means descends to sons and grandsons (to posterity).

No individual or a company has got the right to cause pollution and spoil the environment of the area. Strength should be used to uphold justice.

A company should use all its power and money to provide welfare measures to the people of the surrounding area. This is not only a social responsibility but social justice. The Sanskrit texts lay emphasis on *dharma* in every endeavour. The word *dharma* is an all-encompassing term. It refers to justice, truth, responsibility, duty and virtue. A company also has to follow its *dharma*. That particular *dharma* includes social obligation and responsibility towards owners of the company, employees, shareholders, customers, suppliers, dealers, government, competitors and the entire society. A company's *dharma* also includes all aspects of business ethics. If the concept of *dharma* is understood by all sections of the society, the entire country will prosper.

11

Total Quality Management

LIKE all sciences, the management science has also made rapid strides in the last few decades. The revolution in the information technology has made an impact on management science as well. The three *mantras* of the modern era, viz. liberalization, privatization and globalization have brought about wholesale changes in management concepts. The reality of facing worldwide competition has made companies think about quality orientation in their products. Gone are the days of monopolistic tendencies. Earlier, people were wedded to certain brands and products, but today people do not hesitate to change their favourite brand if a better quality product is available for the same price. In fact, people are ready to spend a little more if better quality stuff is available. Accordingly a new principle has emerged in the business circles, namely, Total Quality Management (TQM).

What is TQM?

The TQM comes in something like a package. The main idea is to meet consumer requirements and achieve customer satisfaction. Customer satisfaction can be achieved only by maintaining a high standard of quality. Quality is not a flash from the pan. It is a continuous process and therefore, companies have to look for continuous maintenance of standard through effective management policies. The conscious approach towards better quality should come from grassroot level, that is, from the workers' level in a company. The TQM consists of all these factors, viz.

(i) Achieving customer satisfaction through maintenance of quality,

(ii) Bring about the necessary changes in the product so as to meet the demands of the customer,

(iii) Evolving a process by which a high standard is maintained continuously, and

(iv) Create an awareness of quality at the grassroot level, that is, among all the workers and all the employees.

This is a fast changing world. The notion of quality also keeps changing. Earlier, people were satisfied with a soap that gave a good lather. Now people look for other aspects like good fragrance and skin friendliness/suitability. Therefore, there are special soaps for rough skin, soft skin, oily skin and so on. People look for such specialized care. A company has to keep pace with such changes in the tastes of people. Moreover, today, there are several agencies to judge the quality of products; quality certification agencies like ISO-9000 have also come into existence. TQM takes into account all these aspects.

The Features of TQM

ACHIEVING CUSTOMER SATISFACTION THROUGH MAINTENANCE OF QUALITY

It used to be a sellers' market, a few years ago. Now there is a shift toward customer orientation. Knowledge explosion and spread of education have brought about large-scale changes in the attitudes of people. Now companies are forced to mention the ingredients of the product, date of manufacture, etc. People read them and decide whether a particular product is good for them or not. People are not carried away by advertisements. A few years back there was high-pressure advertisement for a particular brand of soap powder which was also very cheap, price-wise. But people rejected it on the ground of poor quality. So companies have realized that, in order to stay in the market, they have to maintain the quality of the product.

BRINGING ABOUT NECESSARY CHANGES IN THE PRODUCT SO AS TO MEET THE DEMANDS OF THE CUSTOMER

The demands of the customers keep changing, it may be with reference to the quality, size (or quantity) or even packing material. A company has to make an assessment of the demands of the customer and make necessary changes in the product itself. For example a soap manufacturer may add a herbal component in the product in keeping with the demands of the customers. A product may even need pruning of its size. For example, Lifebuoy soap used to come in a big rectangular shape. One found it rather difficult to handle it. Now the same product comes in a handy size. Complan, originally had only one flavour. Then it introduced chocolate flavour since majority of the consumers are children. There are tea products mixed with cardamom flavour. A number of products come with different varieties or flavours in order to cater to the needs of different sections of people. Oil manufacturers concentrate on low fat content in their product. Some companies produce diabetic special products. All these are based on customer requirements.

CONTINUOUS MAINTENANCE OF STANDARD

Newly started hotels will generally maintain a good standard in the beginning. After some time, when it is sure of a set of regular customers, the quality will slowly go down. The trend has changed now. People are quick to judge the standard and change their choice of the product or the brand. Customers expect continuous maintenance of standard and continuous improvement as well. In the wake of stiff competition, continuous improvement has become a necessity. People are now ready to pay a little more for improved standard of a product. But the onus is now on the companies to convince people of the improved standard of their products.

CREATING AN AWARENESS AMONG EMPLOYEES

The TQM concept has to be spread among all sections of the employees to achieve the full purpose it. Employees are generally addicted to routine work. They resist change but if they are told about the significance of the change, they will accept it. Unless they are convinced about the need for the change, the product will remain the same. New machines, separate training, different kinds of raw material and the like may be needed when improvement of quality in the product is envisaged. Unless the employees concerned are involved in the process, it will be difficult to achieve TQM.

The 14-Point Charter of Deming

W. Edwards Deming, one of the pioneers in the field of quality management, proposed a guideline for top managers.[1] They are:

(i) Create constancy of purpose for improvement of product and service.

(ii) Adopt the new philosophy that ever-increasing quality is necessary for corporate survival.

(iii) Catch the errors at source and rectify.

---

1. Quality, productivity and competitive positions, Cambridge Massachusetts Institute of Technology Centre for Advanced Engineering Study, 1982.

(iv) End the practice of awarding business on price tag alone.

(v) Constantly and for ever improve the system of production and service.

(vi) Institute modern methods of training on the job.

(vii) Institute leadership training.

(viii) Drive out fear.

(ix) Breakdown barriers between staff areas.

(x) Eliminate slogans, exhortations and targets for workspace.

(xi) Eliminate numerical quotas.

(xii) Remove barriers to pride of workmanship.

(xiii) Institute vigorous programme of education and training.

(xiv) Take action to accomplish the transformation.

Deming advocates systems approach to realize the objective of TQM. A system is a series of functions or activities, all of which are geared up together for realizing the objectives of an organization. In other words, the materials, machinery, the methods and the manpower must be oriented towards quality, in order to achieve TQM.

For achieving TQM, the managers are advised to look beyond things. Managers should look beyond power centres and think of decentralization. They may even go one step further and plan for empowerment of employees. Such a step is bound to kindle the imagination and originality of the employees. One should even look beyond empowerment and turn every job into business. An employee should not have the impression that he/she is doing a job for somebody. He/

She should rather be made to feel that he/she is doing a business of his/her own. Employees must be made to feel that they are independent contractors of a particular job. Opportunities should be given for them also to do the corporate talk. The managers should look beyond change and think of bringing about perpetual revolution.

Help from Sanskrit Sources in Achieving TQM

TQM speaks of continuous maintenance of highest standard and continuous improvement of quality at all levels. For the sake of convenience, let us take one aspect, namely, the product. Granting that one should aim at continuous improvement of the quality of the product, where do we end up? If we imagine that 1 per cent improvement is contributed everyday, in 100 days we would have achieved 100 per cent improvement. So it must end there. From the 101st day, there cannot be any further improvement. Apparently, this theory seems to be correct. But there is a fallacy. From the level of 1st day's product the 100th day product is perfect. But keeping the 100th day product as the basis, continuous improvement is possible. Thus it goes on endlessly. What is the ultimate quality of the product? It will be as perfect as the Supreme Being himself who is the creator and sustainer of the entire universe. The Viśiṣṭādvaita philosophy has a point here. All the products are part of the world or matter. All the living beings come under the concept of *jīva*. The matter and *jīva* are the products of the God Almighty. Matter and *jīva* are the body of that Supreme Soul. This is called *śarīra — śarīrī bhāva*. God is the substance or the *summum bonum* of the universe and hence he is called *prakārī*. The *jīva* and the matter are *prakāra*s or modes. They are only projections of god and have no existence apart from the substance. For example, ocean is but a reservoir of water. There are also waves in it. But the wave has no separate existence from the water of the ocean. It is only a projection of water and is indivisible from it. Hence, the relationship, is called *prakārī-prakāra bhāva.*

In another sense, God is the master; the *jīva* and the matter are subordinate to it. They exist for the use and purpose of the master. They are subservient to the master. There are a lot of responsibilities for a master. The servants working under a benevolent master will be happy to remain as servants, since all their needs are looked after by the master. The master is called *śeṣi*; the *jīva* and the matter are called *śeṣa*s. The relationship between the two is called *śeṣa-śeṣi bhāva*. The *śeṣa*s derive supreme joy is being subservient to the *śeṣi*. They find the real meaning of their existence in such a realization.

In a company, there are materials like the wheels, bolts, nuts, shifts, belts, etc. All their functions are different. But once united, they together get transformed into a machine. Once connected to power, the machine starts working. If all the components are viewed as products of God, there will be a conscious effort to make them as perfect as possible, just as the best fruits and flowers are chosen and offered to God. So the products produced will be of better quality than those produced mechanically. Similarly, if every employee thinks that he/she is doing a job assigned to him/her by God, his/her work will be a quality work.

One of the important tenets of Viśiṣṭādvaita philosophy is *bhakti* or devotion to God. The sole requisite for *bhakti* is sincerity. One may offer just a fruit or a flower or just a leaf or a little water. But if it is offered with a pure heart, God accepts it. The Lord says in the *Gītā*, "Whatever you do, whatever you eat, whatever you offer in sacrifice, whatever you give in charity, whatever austerity you perform — do that as an offering unto me." If a work is done with such a feeling, that is, as an offering to God, it will definitely be a high-quality work. God's devotees are fourfold — *ārtta* (one seeking relief from misery), *jijñāsu* (one in quest of the supreme soul), *arthārthī* (one seeking some fulfilment of worldly objects) and *jñānī* (one with supreme knowledge). Among them, *arthārthī* is involved in the work of several kinds in this world. But he/she sees God through his/her work; for him/her work is worship. Naturally, there is quality in his/her work. So, for a person seeking emancipation or communion with God, it is not absolutely necessary to sit in a temple and do worship all the time forgetting regular duties. One can attain the same state by seeing the work as work of God, by putting one's heart and soul into it and by aiming at highest quality in the works. A thing of beauty is a joy for ever. Similarly, a perfect work or a high-quality work is a source of joy. A teacher derives immense pleasure when a student trained by him/her scores 100 per cent in the subject taught by him/her. Likewise the employees must be taught to derive such kind of a joy by achieving highest quality in their work. If this is realized then there is TQM.

Actions done with evenness of mind which consists in the renunciation of the main result and with equanimity towards success or failure in respect of the secondary results, lead to perfection in work. In the march towards quality, a lot of Research and Development work may be needed. The success or failure of the attempts should not bother us. If it bothers, the attempt to achieve quality will suffer. Similarly, the main result, namely, the profit may not be substantial in spite of increased quality of the product. It could even be loss. But profit or loss should not deter us from achieving quality. Hence, the *Gītā* says:

दूरेण ह्यवरं कर्म बुद्धियोगाद्धनञ्जय।
बुद्धौ शरणमन्विच्छ कृपणाः फलहेतवः।।

dūreṇa hyavaraṁ karma buddhiyogāddhanañjaya ।
buddhau śaraṇam anviccha kṛpaṇāḥ phalahetavaḥ ।।
— *Bhagavad-Gītā*, II.49

Action with attachment is far inferior to action done with evenness of mind. Seek refuge in evenness of mind. Miserable are they who act with a motive for results.

A person who is established in evenness of mind in the performance of actions, relinquishes good and evil actions which cause bondage. He/She will be in a state of freedom always. Freedom always brings out the best in a person. Such kind of freedom is fundamental to TQM.

The *Gītā* speaks of the qualities of a *sthitaprajña*. A *sthitaprajña* is defined thus:

दुःखेष्वनुद्विग्नमनाः सुखेषु विगतस्पृहः।
वीतरागभयः क्रोधः स्थितधीर्मुनिरुच्यते।।

duḥkheṣvanudvigna manāḥ sukhesu vigataspṛhaḥ ।
vītarāgabhayaḥ krodhaḥ sthitadhīr munirucyate ।।
— *Bhagavad-Gītā*, II.56

He whose mind is not perturbed in pain, who has no longing for pleasures, who is free from desires, fear and anger is called a sage of firm wisdom.

A person rooted in firm wisdom will not have any longing for enjoyment of worldly pleasures, that is, even though the things which he/she likes are near him/her, he/she has no longing for them. He/She is free from desire and anger; desire is longing for objects not yet obtained; he/she is free from this. Fear is the affliction produced when undesirable persons or things are met. Anger is a disturbed state of mind that is aimed at another sentient being who is the cause of confrontation with what is not desirable. Desire, fear and anger are the causes of imperfection in us. They prevent us from producing perfect things. So a bit of training for the employees in overcoming craving desires, anger and fear will go a long way in achieving TQM.

The next point is, how to overcome them? Let us take, for example, the desire; desires generally arise towards persons or objects. With respect to desire towards objects, two forces act on us — (i) the power of the objects themselves, and (ii) the attachment that our mind develops toward the objects. In order to overcome desire, one has to withstand the onslaught of the sense objects and also control the mind from getting itself attached to them. It is a difficult process but one has to start practising it for ultimate peace. It is very important to control desire because uncontrolled desire leads to further complications. For example, if the desired object is not attained, there arises anger in the mind.

Anger leads to delusion; delusion leads to loss of memory which in turn leads to the loss of the power of discrimination. The loss of power of discrimination lands us in total destruction, says the *Gītā*.

ध्यायतो विषयान् पुंसः सङ्गस्तेषूपजायते।
सङ्गात् सञ्जायते कामः कामात् क्रोधोऽभिजायते।
क्रोधाद्भवति संमोहः संमोहात् स्मृतिविभ्रमः।
स्मृतिभ्रंशात्-बुद्धिनाशः बुद्धिनाशात् प्रणश्यति॥

dhyāyato viṣayān puṁsaḥ saṅgasteṣūpajāyate।
saṅgāt sañjāyate kāmaḥ kāmāt krodho 'bhijāyate॥
krodhād bhavati saṁmohaḥ saṁmohāt smṛtivibhramaḥ।
smṛtibhraṁśāt buddhināśaḥ budhināśāt praṇaśyati॥

— II.62-63

So we must strike at the root cause, that is, the very thought of worldly attractions must be rooted out of the mind. A person, with his/her mind set on other things, will not be able to focus on the work on hand and hence the quality will suffer.

Unless the mind is at peace, quality in the work cannot be achieved. How to get peace of mind? The *Gītā* says,

> विहाय कामान् यस्सर्वान् पुमांश्चरति निःस्पृहः।
> निर्ममो निरहङ्कारः स शान्तिमधिगच्छति॥
>
> *vihāya kāmān yaḥ sarvān pumāṁścarati niḥspṛhaḥ*।
> *nirmamo nirahaṅkāraḥ sa śāntimadhigacchati*॥
>
> — II.71

> The man who abandoning all desires, abides without longing and possession and the sense of "I" and "Mine" wins peace.

The scriptural texts prescribe another method for achieving perfection in work. They say, "Do not consider it as your work. Think that it is God's work. Then you can achieve perfection in it. Dedicate every work and its results to God." The Gītā says:

> मयि सर्वाणि कर्माणि संन्यस्याध्यात्मचेतसा।
> निराशीर्निर्ममो भूत्वा युध्यस्व विगतज्वरः॥
>
> *mayi sarvāṇi karmāṇi saṁnyasyādhyātmacetasā*।
> *nirāśīrnirmamo bhūtvā yudhyasva vigatajvaraḥ*॥
>
> — III.30

> Surrendering all your actions to me, with a mind focused on the self, free from desire and selfishness, fight with the heat of excitement abated.

The principles enunciated by the *Gītā* on *karma* or action lead not only to quality in the work but also that in entire life. This is indeed TQM.

12

Conclusion

A COMPARATIVE study of the principles of management and Sanskrit literature is a fascinating subject since one finds related ideas in both. It may also be pointed out that no subject is too old or too modern. Seeds of modern subjects are found embedded in ancient literature and older ideas on human psychology are still relevant in the light of modern research. We have seen that the texts like *Arthaśāstra* and *Bhagavad-Gītā* are quite useful to the present-day managers in understanding the value of human capital and in channelizing it for the benefit of the society.

The trend in industry has changed from product orientation to customer orientation. The values of the customer and customer satisfaction have assumed a greater dimension on account of opening up of trade and globalization. The next point is that companies cannot be concentrating only on their profit. They have to take upon themselves the social responsibility of elevating the society economically and educationally. Business ethics has become an important subject in management studies. Moreover, people have become more knowledgeable. They are not only looking for the product and the price but they have become quality conscious as well. People not only took at the products manufactured by a company but also at what the company stands for, what its mission and vision are and what are the values for which it stands. It is a matter of common experience that everyone wants to get something positive out of whatever one has or buys and also avoid whatever has a negative impact on oneself. A person attaches a value to a thing if it satisfies his/her desire or the achievement of ends as a result of the knowledge about it. It is the cognition of the facts about an object that leads to the realization of value, through arousing a desire for it. It is also possible that the desire is goaded by an idea of the value to be realized (*phalecchāṁ prati phala-jñānaṁ kāraṇam*).[1]

Quality consciousness is natural to all human beings. It becomes important once the basic needs are satisfied. For example, when a person is very hungry, he/she does not mind about the quality. He/She first quenches his/her hunger by taking whatever is available. But once hunger is subsided, he/she looks for quality. Then he/she begins to attach higher values like "right means" and "true value" to the quality he/she looks for, though he/she does not abandon lower values like self-preservation and race preservation. The Sanskrit texts come up with an illustration here. Though growing in the quagmire, the lotus looks pure and bright.

Though the value of "values" differs from person to person and place to place, there are certain basic values that are acceptable to all people. So "desirability" alone cannot determine the importance of value. What is desired may not be beneficial.[2] The *Kaṭha Upaniṣad,* therefore, speaks of *preyas* (what is desirable) and *śreyas* (what is beneficial). So a good manager may not emphasize on what is *preyas,* that is, what is desired by people. He/She has to think of what is beneficial for them, that is, quality.

---

1. *Siddhānta Muktāvalī,* p. 467.
2. *Kaṭha Upaniṣad,* I.ii.1-3.

The ritual texts emphasize this particular aspect. Many of the rituals are performed either for the sake of the children or for the sake of other family members. There are certain longer sacrifices that are performed for the benefit of the entire society. The action is done by one but the benefit goes to the others. This is a *dharma*. Such a *dharma* is fundamental to social consciousness that is expected of a company.

Once it is decided what values are to be followed, it is necessary to draft a resolution on the means for the realization of the values concerned. The end is thought of first but the means to achieve it is equally important. The Sanskrit texts emphasize that both the end and the means are to be noble. The end does not justify the means. This will be a very useful hint for a modern manager in planning his/her activities. In the execution part of it, the means come first and the mission is achieved at the end; and so, the values must be thought of first before embarking on an endeavour. The idea of value serves as the social cause. And therefore the Nyāya texts speak of *iṣṭa sādhanatā jñāna* (knowledge of the right means of the desired goal) and *kṛti sādhyatā jñāna* (knowledge of the possibility of achievement within the sphere of *dharma*).

Some of the theories of Indian philosophy may be useful in understanding the human nature especially when we study the organizational behaviour. Almost all the systems. Indian philosophy recognize the existence of a conscious subject, the *jīva*, in every human body. This fundamental concept is indispensable for understanding the nature of human experience. Indian thinkers distinguish this *jīva*, the empirical self from the metaphysical self. What restricts the empirical self is the *manas* or the mind. Though it is a limiting adjunct for the *jīva*, it is also instrumental in the realization of the higher goals attempted by the self. *Jñāna* or knowledge is the basis of all activities of a human being. The Nyāya-Vaiśeṣika schools hold that knowledge is a specific quality of the self. Kumārila, a great Mīmāṁsaka, considers knowledge as a process taking place in the *jīva*. According to another view, knowledge is a revelation of the consciousness of the self. The function of knowledge is to reveal objects to the self. Objects may be known directly or indirectly through a psychic medium. All knowledge that is got from the instrument like the eye may not be valid. There could also be invalid knowledge as one assumes a rope to be a serpent. In order to get correct knowledge one may depend on the *pramāṇa*s or means of valid knowledge. Valid knowledge is that which is not negated by one or the other of the *pramāṇa*s. Majority of the schools accept *pratyakṣa* (perception), *anumāna* (inference) and *śabda* (verbal testimony).

The term *dharma* has already been referred to in the earlier chapter. Now a question arises. How to ascertain *dharma*? It is pointed out that *dharma* is to be known through verbal testimony. There are also two other criteria that guide the knowledge of *dharma*. They are (i) custom (*ācāra*) and (ii) self-satisfaction or feeling at peace with oneself (*ātma-tuṣṭi*). *Dharma* may vary according to the custom that is prevailing from place to place; in other words, *dharma* needs social approval; but *ātma-tuṣṭi* requires self-approval. So Kālidāsa says:

सतां हि सन्देहपदेषु वस्तुषु।
प्रमाणमन्तः करण प्रवृत्तयः।।

satām hi sandehapadeṣu vastuṣu।
pramāṇamantaḥkaraṇa pravr̥ttayaḥ।।
— *Abhijñānaśākuntalam*, I.22

To the good, their own conscience is a sure guide in matters of doubt.

At the same time, what the conscience says should not come into conflict with the accepted verbal testimony. Hence, the conscience should stand for the moral insight, which is necessary in matters of minute details about which accepted codes and the practice of elders are silent.

The concept that goes hand in hand with *dharma* is *karma*, about which again some reference has already been made. The *karma* theory satisfactorily explains the causes of things that happen in the world.[3] It signifies that nothing can happen without a cause. All our pleasures and pains, trials and tribulations, ups and downs are causes of our own *karma*, that is, our own actions done previously (in this or previous births). It also gives hope for future. You are the maker of your own destiny. You reap what you sow. So, watch your actions. If they are good, your future is bound to be good. The *karma* theory may act as an eye-opener for the managers. If an employee commits a mistake as a consequence of some initial disposition or through the force of congenital impulses (*prakṛteḥ svabhāvāt*), it is expected of the managers to judge him leniently, instead of blaming him outright. A question may arise here. If everything is decided by our *karma*, then don't we have any independence at all? Perhaps not, with respect to our past actions. But we do have independence to decide our course of action for the present in anticipation of their results in future. Freedom does not mean "gay abandon" and reckless actions. Freedom does not mean "free for all." I have the freedom to walk on the road, but I have no freedom to obstruct the path of another. Unrestricted freedom has no relevance. Freedom does not mean total absence of determination either. Along with freedom comes responsibility. Every *karma* that we do leads to double result. First, we experience the result of the

---

3. Hirianna, M., *Indian Conception of Values.*

deeds that we have performed; it could be pleasure or pain. Second, they leave behind a memory in us. Seeing the result of the deed performed earlier, we may repeat it or desist from doing it. The first experience of touching fire leaves behind an impression for the entire life. We will never touch it again.

A question may arise here. If *karma* is so powerful as to decide our present and future, what is the role of God? Does He helplessly watch people enjoying pleasure or pain on account of their *karma*? The Dvaita and Viśiṣṭādvaita schools do not believc so. They say that though *karma* is very powerful, devotion to God can change its course. Being pleased with the sincerity of his devotees, God will mitigate their sufferings. By diverting their thoughts on God, the devotees can forget the suffering though it has come upon them on account of their past deeds.

Side by side with the theory of *karma*, there developed the theory of fate. It is often said that fate cannot be avoided. What is destined to happen will happen. Nobody can stop it. But Sanskrit sources also emphasize that one should not give up one's efforts relying on destiny or luck. Without manly efforts, the destiny will not bring about fruits.

यथा ह्येकेन चक्रेण रथस्य न गतिर्भवेत्।
पुरुषकारेण विना दैवं न सिध्यति।।

yathā hi ekena cakreṇa rathasya na gatirbhavet ।
puruṣakāreṇa vinā daivaṁ na siddhyati ।।
— *Yājñavalkya-Smṛti*, I.351

Just as the movement of a chariot does not take place with a single wheel so destiny cannot bring in success without mainly efforts.

This particular concept will be very helpful in moulding the attitudes of workers in a company. A slightly modified dictum will be very useful in motivating the employees. The management is ready to help them. But there should be a conscious effort on the part of the employees to contribute to the growth of the company by their sincere work.

So *karma* is only one of the factors that determine the course of events in our life. It may be a dominant factor, but it is not the sole one. It may be an unseen factor but it may not be all powerful. One's own efforts, if sufficiently strong, may overwhelm the influence of the unseen factor. There is a *subhāṣita* which says:

उद्योगिनं पुरुषसिंहमुपैति लक्ष्मी:
दैवेन देयमिति कापुरुषा वदन्ति।
दैवं निहत्य कुरु पौरुषमात्मशक्त्या
यत्ने कृते यदि न सिद्ध्यति कोऽत्र दोष:।।

udyoginaṁ puruṣasiṁhamupaiti lakṣmīḥ
daivena deyamiti kāpuruṣā vadanti ।
daivaṁ nihatya kuru pauruṣamātma-śaktyā
yatne kṛte yadi na siddhyati kot 'ra doṣaḥ ।।
— *Ghaṭakarpara-Nīti*, v.20, p.83

Prosperity attends on the lion of a man who puts in his best efforts. Only mean people say that it should be given by destiny. Dismiss the notion of destiny and do your efforts with the power of your conscious self. In spite of your efforts, if success does not attend on you, where is the defect?

The Sanskrit sources prescribe the "duties" for people following several walks of life. Four types of duties are generally recognized. They are:

(i) *nitya karma* (obligatory duties),
(ii) *kāmya karma* (optional deeds),
(iii) *naimittika karma* (occasional duties), and
(iv) *pratiṣiddha karma* (prohibited actions)

We need not go into the details since they can be brought under just two heads namely, general duties and special duties.

A list of general duties is given by Manu. They are contentment, forbearance, gentleness, respect for other's property, cleanliness, self-control, knowledge, wisdom, veracity and patience.

धृतिः क्षमा दमोऽस्तेयं शौचमिन्द्रियनिग्रहः।
दानं दमो दया क्षान्तिः सर्वेषां धर्म-साधनम्॥

dhṛtiḥ kṣamā damo 'steyaṁ śaucamindriya-nigrahaḥ ।
dānaṁ damo dayā kṣāntiḥ sarveṣāṁ dharma sādhanam ॥

— Manu, VI.92

We may see that several of these when practised by us have an influence on others as well. For example, when non-violence is practised, it brings about a change of attitude in others. Some of the duties are obligatory. For example, we have to help a person in distress, otherwise we will be adding to his injury.

Special duties are those that pertain to a particular profession. For example, it is the duty of a warrior to fight and kill the enemies. If differs from the general duty of non-violence. But in the interest of the nation, the warrior has to do his special duty of killing the enemies. A good knowledge of general duties and special duties will definitely help all sections of an organization.

Sanskrit works on literary criticism have made original contribution on aesthetics. They primarily point out how literature becomes enjoyable and equate this joy to the ultimate joy of the liberated state. One must be able to enjoy beauties of nature. But the realization of the intrinsic beauty of nature means, once again, the possession of right knowledge acquired through self-discipline. It is the imagination and creativity that add beauty to a piece of work. Thus a poet would describe the moon as the lotus that has grown in the waters of the heavenly Ganges. In an organization, the employees may be encouraged to love their work as a piece of art. It may help them to show creativity and innovation in their work. In some organizations, gentle music is relayed from a centralized system. It helps the employees to lower their tension, break the monotony and work with vigour and energy.

The highest class of poetry is that which has suggestive element in it. Anything that is expressed openly may look crude. If the same idea is put in a suggestive way it will be appealing and also beautiful. Thus a girl would say to her lover who is about to depart, "You may go through the usual forest route. A dog which was troubling the travellers has been killed by the lion roaming in that area." The lover got the hint and stayed back. Here the expressed sense was "go" but the suggestive meaning, namely, "do not go" became more powerful since the lover stayed back. Some amount of suggestive element in communication will be helpful in driving home a point effectively. It will be particularly helpful in the business circles. When an employee is to be taken to task, direct and harsh words may wound his/her feelings. On the other hand, suggestive expressions will have a better effect on him/her.

A study of Sanskrit literature, as pointed out in the present work, will be of immense help to all sections of an organization. The purpose of the present work is to unite both the ancient and the modern subjects and strike a balance between them. It is not peculiar to Sanskrit literature alone. Similar such studies could be made with reference to Tamil literature or English literature. Synthesis and analysis are two important aspects of any scientific study. By integrating two diverse subjects like management and Sanskrit literature, one gets a deeper vision and a broader perspective. Great scholars have integrated science and humanity, particularly philosophy, and have found that both have a meeting point. Where physics ends, metaphysics begins. A true scholar will not find any subject as alien to him. This could probably be another interpretation of the famous stanza,

> अयं निजः परोवेति गणना लघुचेतसाम्।
> उदारचरितानां तु वसुधैव कुटुम्बकम्॥
>
> *ayaṁ nijaḥ paroveti gaṇanā laghu cetasām* ।
> *udāracaritānāṁ tu vasudhaiva kuṭumbakam* ॥
> — *Śārṅgadharapaddhati*, v.273

> It is only the narrow minded people who consider "this" as belonging to them and "the other" as lying outside their contention. For broad minded people, the entire world is their family.

All studies, whether independent or comparative, add to the storehouse of knowledge. It is hoped that the present work will be one more small step taken in this direction. A study of ancient literature will make the managers better managers and the workers better workers. It will bring about a positive change in the attitude of all sections of the people. With such an optimistic mind, we will be able to see a better world tomorrow. Let mutual suspicion and quarrels end. Let there be peace and harmony everywhere. *Sarve janāḥ sukhino bhavantu.*

Bibliography

Sanskrit Works

Abhijñānaśākuntalam of Kālidāsa, ed., M.R. Kale, Delhi: Motilal Banarsidass, 1994.

Arthaśāstra of Kauṭilya, ed. R.P. Kangle, Delhi: Motilal Banarsidass, 1986.

Bhagavad-Gītā, ed. Swami Chidbhavananda, Sri Ramakrishna Tapovanam, Tiruppurittura, 1972.

Bhāsanāṭakacakra, ed. C.R. Devadhar, Delhi: Motilal Banarsidass, 1999.

Dhvanyāloka of Ānanda Vardhana, ed. K. Krishnamurthy, Dharvar: Karnatak University, 1974.

Ghaṭakarpara Nīti, Kashmir Sanskrit Series, 1921.

Hitopadeśa of Nārāyaṇa Paṇḍita, ed. M.R. Kale, Delhi: Motilal Banarsidass, 1980.

Īśādi Daśopaniṣad, Delhi: Motilal Banarsidass, 1992.

Kādambarī of Bāṇa, ed. M.R. Kale, Delhi: Motilal Banarsidass, 1968.

Kāmandakīya Nīti, Trivandrum: Trivandrum Sanskrit Series, no.14.

Kaṭhopaniṣad, ed. Swami Sarvananda, Chennai: Sri Ramakrishna Math, 2000.

Kirātārjunīya of Bhāravi, Varanasi: Chowkambha Sanskrit Series, 1999.

Kumārasambhava, Bombay: N.S. Press, 1955.

Mahābhārata, Pune: The Chitrasala Press, 1929-33.

Mahābhārata, Mahābhārata Condensed, ed. A.M. Srinivasachariar, Chennai: G.A. Natesan, 1935.

Mālavikāgnimitra, Works of Kālidāsa-I, (ed.) C.R. Devadhar, Delhi: Motilal Banarsidass, 1977.

Manusmṛti, Bombay: N.S. Press, 1914.

Mṛcchakaṭika of Śūdraka, Delhi: Motilal Banarsidass, 1972.

Pañcatantra, Delhi: Motilal Banarsidass, 1969.

Raghuvaṁśa, Bombay: N.S. Press, 1920.

Ratnāvalī of Śrīharṣa, Bombay: N.S. Press, 1913.

Ṛgveda, ed. H.H. Griffth, Delhi: Motilal Banarsidass, 1995.

Śārṅgadharapaddhati, ed. P. Peteron, London, 1888.

Śatakatraya of Bhartṛhari, Varanasi: Chowkambha, 1998.

Siddhānta Muktāvalī, Bombay: N.S. Press, 1916.

Śiśupālavadha of Māgha, Bombay: Gopal Narayan, 1932.

Subhāṣita Ratna Bhāṇḍāgāra, Delhi: Chowkambha, 1991.

Tarkasaṁgraha of Annambhaṭṭa, Chennai: Sri Ramakrishna Math, 1985.

Uttararāmacaritam, ed. G.K. Bhatt, Surat: Popular Publishing House, 1965.

Vākyapadīya, Trivandrum: University Manuscripts Library, 1943.

Vālmīki Rāmāyaṇa, Gorakhpur: Gita Press, 1998.

Vedānta Paribhāṣā, Kolkata: Advaita Ashrama, Ramakrishna Math.

Vidura-Nīti, ed. P.N. Menon, Palghat: The Educational Supplies Depot, 1962.

Yājñavalkya-Smṛiti, Bombay: N.S. Press, 1926.

Other Works

Albanese, Robert, *Management Toward Accountability and Performance*, Richard D. Irwin, Illinois: Homewood, 1973.

Alford and Beathy, *Management*, New York: Macmillan, 1976.

Allen, L.A., *Management and Organisation*, Tokyo: McGraw-Hill, 1978.

———, *Professional Management*, New York: McGraw-Hill, 1976.

Armstrong, M., *Handbook of Personnel Management Practice*, Paga: Kogan, 1977.

Beach, Dale, S., *Personnel — The Management of People at Work*, London: Collier Macmillan, 1965.

Dalton, E. McFarland, *Management Foundations and Practices*, New York: Macmillan, 1979.

Drucker, Peter F., *The Practice of Management*, London: Mercury Books, 1961-62.

Flippo, E.B., and Munninger, G.M., *Management*, New York: Allen & Bacon, 1978.

Freud, Sigmund, *An Outline of Psychology* (tr. J. Strachery), New York: W.W. Norton and Company, 1959.

Gleuck, W.F., *Management*, Illinois: The Dryden Press, Hindsdale, 1977.

Gopala Iyengar, V., *First Book of Sanskrit*, Tanjore, 1959.

Haynes & Massie, *Essentials of Management*, Prentice Hall International Eaglewood Cliffs, N.J. 1973.

Hersey, Paul, K.H. Blanchard, *Management of Organisational Behaviour*, Prentice Hall, Eaglewood Cliffs, 1977.

Hirianna, M., *Indian Conception of Values*, Mysore: Kavyalaya Publishers, 1975.

Hudson, C.L., *Business Organisation and Operation*, London: Staple Press, 1970.

Jung, Carl, *Analytical Psychology*, in Psychology of Personality, Readings in Theory, ed. William S. Sahakian, Rand McNelly, Chicago, 1965.

Keith Davis, *Human Behaviour of Work*, New Delhi: Tata McGraw-Hill, 1975.

Koontz, Harold, Cyril O'Donnell, *Elements of Management*, New Delhi: Tata-McGraw-Hill, 1975.

Koontz, Harold and O'Donnell *Essential of Management*, New Delhi: Tata-McGraw-Hill, 1982.

Krishna, G.R., *Indian Ethos for Modern Management*, UBSPD, 1999.

Kunjanni Raja, K., *Indian Theories of Meaning*, Chennai: The Adyar Library and Research Centre, 2000.

Lesikar, R.V. and J.D. Petit, *Business Communication*, D. Irwin Richard, Homewood, Illinois, 1996.

Lopez, Felix M., *The Making of a Manager*, Mumbai: Taraporewala, 1977.

Luthers, Fred, *Organisational Behaviour*, New York: McGraw-Hill, 1977.

Newman, N.H., C.E. Summer, E.K. Warren, *The Process of Management — Concepts Behaviour and Practice*, New Delhi: Prentice Hall of India, 1979.

Ramaratnam, S., *Prahasana in Sanskrit Literature*, Mysore: Kavyalaya Publishers, 1987.

Rao, V.S.P. and P.S. Narayana, *Principles and Practice of Management*, New Delhi: Kornark Publishers, Pvt. Ltd., 1996.

Redfield, C.E., *Communication in Management.* The University of Chicago Press, 2nd, edn. 1954.

Shull Jr. F.A., A.L. Delbecqus, L. Cummings, *Organisational Decision Making,* New York: McGraw-Hill Book Company, 1970.

Simon, H.H., *The New Science of Management Decision,* New York: Harper and Row, 1960.

Srinivasachari, P.N., *Idea of Personality,* Chennai: The Adyar Library, 1951.

Stoner, J.A.F., R.E. Freeman, D.R. Gilbert, *Management,* New Delhi: Prentice Hall of India, 1996.

Swami Ranganathanada, *Universal Message of the Bhagavadgītā* (in 3 vols., Kolkata: Advaita Ashrama, 2001.

Terry, G.R., *Principles of Management,* Richard D. Irwin, Homewood, Illinois, 1968.

Tiruvalluvar's Tirukkural, Tirunelveli: The South Indian Saiva Siddhanta Works Publishing Society, 2000.

Articles and Papers

Calicut University Seminar Papers, Calicut University, 2002, (first nine articles in this list).

"Principles of Management in Nītiśataka" N.V.P. Unithri.

"Management Values and Business Ethics", P.N. Chetty.

"Indian Management Thought — A Way of Life", H.V. Sankaranarayana.

"Sanskrit Resources for Contemporary Problems in Management", C. Rajendran.

"Indian Philosophy and Human Resource Management", K.N.N. Elayath.

"Organisational Transportation Through Values", P. Mohan.

"Bhagavad-Gītā and Modern Management", C.V. Jayamani.

"Bhagavad-Gītā as a Text for Crisis Management", N.V.P. Unithri.

"Ethics in Business Management", N. Ranganathan.

Geisler, E.B., "Manpower Planning, an Emerging Staff Function", *Management Bulletin,* American Management Association, 1982.

Jones, T.M., "Corporate Social Responsibility", *California Management,* Review no. 22, Spring 1980.

Levitt, Theodre, "The Managerial Merry-go-round", Hardward Business Review, July-August, 1974.

Miller, E.C., "Objectives and Standards — An Approach to Planning and Control", American Management Association.

Parket, Robert and Henry Ellbert, "Social Responsibility, the Underlying Factors", *Business Horizons*, August 1975.

"Quality, Productivity and Competitive Positions", Centre for Advanced Engineering Study, Massachusetts Institute of Technology, 1982

Rogers, Carl, "A Theory of Therapy, Personality and Impersonal Relationship as Developed in Client Centered Framework", S. Koch, ed., *Psychology: A Study of Science*, vol. XIII, McGraw Hill Book Company, New York, 1959, p. 200.

Smith, D.H., "A Parsimonious Definition of a Group Toward Conceptual Clarity and Scientific Unity", *Sociological Inquiry*, Spring, 1967, p. 141.

Index